A JOHN CATT PUBLICATION

SUCCESSFUL D
CONVERSAtiONS
IN SCHOOL

Improve your team's performance, behaviour and attitude with kindness and success

SONIA GILL

FOREWORD BY ANDY BUCK

First published 2018, this version 2022

by John Catt Educational Ltd,
15 Riduna Park,
Station Road,
Melton, Woodbridge IP12 1BL

Tel: +44 (0) 1394 389850
Fax: +44 (0) 1394 386893
Email: enquiries@johncatt.com
Website: www.johncatt.com

ISBN: 978 1 911 382 52 2

Set and designed by John Catt Educational Limited

Testimonials

'Holding difficult conversations well is the key to successful leadership and management – this easily read book will be invaluable to both experienced and new managers, as it is full of practical advice and sensible ideas to make those conversations work for you.'

Kim Parnell, Headteacher, Balfour Academy, Chatham

'I've been waiting for Sonia to write this book for a long time! A few years ago, my deputy and I did a training session around having successful difficult conversations. The training itself was hugely helpful and I kept the notes from the session rolled up in my cupboard and still refuse to part from them to this day. Thank you Sonia.'

Rebecca Harris, Headteacher, Stourfield Infants School, Bournemouth

'*Successful Difficult Conversations in School* is an invaluable resource for any school leader who wants to improve the culture of their organisation in order to create truly outstanding teaching and learning. It provides a clear, practical, easy-to-follow guide to tackling tricky conversations in a kind and structured way, ensuring that issues are dealt with in a timely manner rather than being allowed to fester. By following Sonia's tried-and-tested methods, school leaders at all levels can ensure that they maintain their own integrity, reduce HR distractions and enable staff to focus on the children's learning.'

Paul Murphy, Headteacher, Lancasterian Primary School

'Whether you are a head or deputy head, a head of department or Year 3 teacher – this book is an invaluable read. It is full of practical ways to help you, when facing one of 'those' conversations with a colleague or parent, you know in your heart you need to have, but would rather avoid having, because you don't really know what to say or how to say it.'

Nigel Taylor, Headmaster, Amesbury School, Surrey

Dedication

This book is dedicated to my husband Phil.

Dealing with conflict is a path we have trodden together. Conflict is not an easy dynamic to embrace and understand. However, facing conflict creatively brings deep, and long-term gains. You have taken up the challenge, Phil, and I feel so lucky to be married to you; someone who is so willing and dedicated to cultivating a thriving, caring, respectful relationship. That takes effort and work and some pretty difficult conversations!

Thank you for your patience, your perspective and your very broad shoulders in embracing healthy conflict with me. Most of all, thank you for always being true to yourself.

I love you more every day.

Contents

Thank you

There are many people to thank on the journey to creating this book.

The school leaders we've worked with.

A big thank you to all of you. You've shared your challenges with us, welcomed our support, let us watch your difficult conversations and let us push you hard, many times, in order to improve. You've used the skills we've shared and reported your successes. Thank you for making the training such a wonderful experience and thank you for trusting us to help.

The headteachers who reviewed this book.

Nigel, Rebecca, Paul, Kim and Kevin, I can't thank you enough for the time you invested to give me incredibly useful feedback – this book is better for your input.

Team Heads Up.

Whether we have been training in your school or organising future training days, I know Team Heads Up are passionate about supporting schools.

My actors.

Our successful difficult conversations training wouldn't be as powerful without you.

Shiraz, you've been with me from the beginning, helping school leaders have better difficult conversations, providing valuable insight and you've made it fun along the way.

Sophie, you've been so great at working with our school leaders, challenging and supporting them to do better, all within a safe learning space and your feedback has been invaluable.

I've loved every minute working with you both. I don't know how you do what you do, but it is magical!

The engine room of Heads Up.

A big thank you to the hidden members of my team who enable us to support schools every day:

Kay, who looks after our schools and somehow keeps us all organised! Nisha and Phil, who look after our schools, spread the word and let us meet new schools to support.

My trainers.

You work hard to give the very best to our schools every day:

Steve, thank you for your feedback, improvements, commitment and your passion for education.

Natasha, you always make schools sparkle with your delightful enthusiasm alongside your perceptive delivery!

The people who brought this book to life

Diane, you wave your magic wand over my words every time. Thank you.

Alex and the John Catt team, for their hard work and support in bringing this book to life.

Paul Garvey for getting the ball rolling.

Foreword

Having difficult conversations with colleagues is an essential part of the job for many professionals working in schools. Yet when I think back to the early days of my own career as a relatively inexperienced middle leader, too often I would either delay having them or avoid them altogether. Why? The clue is in the name: they really are difficult! I would much rather drop hints or make a jokey comment in the hope that this would do the trick. Sometimes of course this would work. But often it wouldn't. For whatever the reason, the person just wouldn't pick up on the nudge I was trying to give them. Worrying about being overly direct and how colleagues might react was a bit scary; the temptation to just try another nudge was irresistible.

Over time, however, I began to learn the power of the more direct conversation. The one where you give someone the benefit of some authentic feedback that is solely intended to help the individual be more effective at what they do. But it took me a long time to work out how best to manage these conversations. I learnt the hard way that there wasn't much to be gained by hiding behind something or someone when delivering a difficult message; nor that there is little point in trying to help someone solve a problem until they have truly accepted that something needs to change. But this learning took a lot of trial and error and it was a long time before I was anywhere near confident in what I was doing. Reading Susan Scott's seminal work, *Fierce Conversations*, was a source of lots of ideas and practical suggestions, but it didn't always resonate with my school context.

Which is why this book is so helpful. It sees the difficult conversation not as something to be afraid of, but something to help bring about change for the better. Rooted in solid theory and evidence, it gives a school-specific context to exploring the why, the how and the what of having difficult conversations.

Fully acknowledging that these conversations are hard, Sonia Gill takes us through the three core components necessary for success, drawing on a wide range of fields, including transactional analysis, experience from the aviation industry and the power of positive psychology.

The book includes some fascinating tools to help with analysing the degree of difficulty of certain conversations as well as calculating the actual financial cost of not having them! I also love the section that examines the ten things that can easily go wrong in a difficult conversation and what do about them if they happen.

Do read the chapter on how to use the book. It acts as the perfect guide to what you may or may not want to read – just another example of how practical and accessible I think this great handbook is going to be for all of us that care about every pupil getting the very best education they deserve.

Andy Buck
Author, speaker, former headteacher,
MAT MD and director at National College, now MD of #honk and
founder of the Leadership Matters website

Using this book (read me first)

You can read this book cover to cover or you can dip and skip your way through it. This short section is an overview to help you decide how *you* can get the most out of this book.

Who am I to tell you about difficult conversations?
Here, I share my back-story around difficult conversations and how I came to support so many people. I share this so you can see how I built up my knowledge and expertise in this area. If you trust me, then skip ahead!

Section 1 looks at why these conversations are so important and provides some important groundwork to the subject:

- Why we need to have difficult conversations.
- How much conflict costs your school.
- How to decide if you should have a difficult conversation.
- Who should have the conversation.
- When you should have the conversation.

Please note: I don't look at skills to make your difficult conversations easier in this section. If that's what you want to learn about straight away, then skip ahead to Section 2.

Section 2 gets into the nitty-gritty of how to improve your difficult conversations. We look at:

- Starting the conversation.
- Structuring it.
- Managing the emotions.
- Making sure positive action follows.
- Adapting your approach for greater success.

These skills will help you deal with difficult conversations you can plan for and those that land on you without warning.

Section 3 looks at the role successful difficult conversations have in creating a culture of feedback for ongoing school improvement and higher performance.

Activities throughout the book aim to help you extract the most value from your reading and develop your skills.

Successful difficult conversations training – how we help you tells you how we support schools to become successful at mastering difficult conversations.

Please be aware that nothing in this book constitutes legal advice and should not be treated as such. Employment law is a complex area and you should always seek expert advice on legal issues.

I will show you lots of skills and techniques that will serve you well. You will have to exercise your own judgement as to when to use them and I will help you as much as I can with developing this sense. Sadly, I can't give you a 'successful difficult conversations by numbers' book; nothing can fully instruct you in exactly what to do and say in any given situation. You have to make those decisions yourself. There is no such thing as a perfect successful difficult conversation, but there are better ones and my aim is to help you have more of these.

Appendices are included to help you dip back into the book at anytime.

1. Appendix A: Chapter summaries – to help you refer back to key sections.

2. Appendix B: All the activities – in one place for you.

3. Appendix C: A table of figures.

4. Appendix D: A checklist to help you prepare for your difficult conversations.

Who is this book for?

The book is mostly for school leaders who need to have difficult conversations. My examples and case studies are centred around school scenarios. However, the skills are applicable to any difficult conversation. School leaders frequently tell me that they have applied these skills in their personal lives and I often use them myself on my husband! (And he knows it!)

This book is a way for me to reach and support more school leaders. As such, there are activities throughout each chapter and online resources to support you.

I hope that this book will help you have your difficult conversations with less stress and more success.

Who am I to tell you about difficult conversations?

I can't pretend I've always handled conflict well. Even now, I can still get it wrong. I've ranged from totally avoiding conflict to having full-on arguments; neither approach is particularly effective. But then, no one had ever taught me how to have *healthy* conflict and there were no role models around me to learn from; there are very few skilled role models for most of us.

I studied psychology at the University of Nottingham, a subject I relish because it allowed me to learn about human behaviour. From there I became a teacher in my own old junior school. As a newly qualified teacher (NQT), I had a challenging class; however, I adored them. They were my team and, together, we were going to become awesome! Our year together was a steep learning curve for me, but the joy of teaching is seeing how well your class progresses academically and personally. Colleagues say you never forget your first class and I remember mine with great fondness – we all learnt a lot!

I went into teaching to become an educational psychologist but, after a while, this no longer seemed the right path for me. I'd enjoyed being a teacher and could have stayed, but I didn't know what I wanted to be 'when I grew up'. So, while time was on my side, I decided to change tack and was lucky to be selected onto the John Lewis graduate leadership programme. At the time, I don't think I fully appreciated just how lucky I was to join this wonderful business.

The programme was great. You start as a sales assistant and then move on to your first management post (a section manager), where you earn your stripes so that you can eventually become a department manager. There are high expectations of graduate trainees from every angle. I was keen to learn as much as I could, as quickly as possible, so I seized every opportunity available to me. One opportunity I requested was to do a mid-year performance review for a member of our team, a light-touch review to give feedback and suggest areas for improvement.

I was rubbish! While praising her work, I also tried to give some constructive feedback that she needed to hear and take on board. It wasn't onerous feedback but I struggled to express myself clearly. She tried her best to understand what I was saying and although the meeting went well on the surface (there were no tears or tantrums), I knew I failed to communicate with clarity. I felt flat. I went home, sat at my kitchen table and realised I had let her down. She wanted to do her job well, to be a great member of the team and I hadn't helped her. If anything, I had confused her and set her off on the wrong path. This was my moment of realisation: if I was going be any good as a leader, one of the skills I had to learn was how to competently deliver difficult messages and much-needed feedback. I had to master this skill so I could support the people in my team to be even better.

Thankfully, John Lewis was an organisation that was (and still is) very much about developing people. I read books, took every training opportunity they offered on difficult conversations and volunteered for as many difficult conversations as I could. I must have seemed crazy, but I knew that I had to put what I was learning into practice. I developed in many ways (and I'm still doing that). My main focus was always my team, as it had been with my class. The question I constantly asked myself was 'How could I help them do better in their role and how could I lead them better?'

And my efforts seemed to work as I progressed quickly at John Lewis. Less than three years after joining the company, I was promoted to the steering group at one of the largest branches, reporting directly to the managing director. Later, I was promoted to another steering group position, opening a new shop, and then went on to lead a team in head office.

I was far from perfect, and I'm still trying to get things right! I don't know about you but I feel that leadership is a series of mistakes that help you improve further. However, no matter how much you get right, there are always more mistakes to be made! A famous saying, attributed to Churchill, motivates me through the bumpy process without losing heart.

'Success consists of going from failure to failure
without loss of enthusiasm.'

I simply keep trying, learning, improving, failing and learning. Repeatedly. As they say:

If we're not making mistakes we're not learning.

I wish it wasn't that way, but it is.

I am passionate about healthy conflict: the good, helpful conflict that improves our personal and professional relationships. This skill is critical in creating higher performance. This skill is critical in creating higher performance because it lets us discuss and improve, without blame or fault-finding.

For me, a difficult conversation is an act of kindness to one another. When I have a difficult conversation with someone, it's because I want the best for them. My underlying message is:

'I care about you enough to tell you something I think you need to know, something that others might not tell you because conflict is uncomfortable. I respect you enough to tell you instead of talking to others about it. I'm willing to put myself in a difficult position to tell you this, to risk you not liking me. I'm willing to spend time thinking about how to tell you this with kindness. I care about you enough, as a person, to do this, because I want you to do as well as you can.'

When someone gives me a difficult message I try to keep this same frame of mind, despite my inevitable, immediate, emotional reaction. I remind myself that this person is giving me a gift of information that I might otherwise not have had. How kind is that?

I founded Heads Up in 2011 to help schools create high-performing cultures by equipping leaders with the skills they need to achieve this. Successful difficult conversations, which are essentially feedback conversations, are vital to high performance. It is the skill schools most often ask us to train them in and it makes the biggest immediate impact on creating a high-performing culture. That is why I've written this book.

I hope this book will help even more school leaders like you have those difficult conversations with greater success and less stress. I hope it will help your team become higher performing and help those who are struggling to improve become an inspiring success story!

Section 1

Why you should have difficult conversations

Chapter 1: Conflict is crucial for great schools

In this chapter, we look at:
· The definition of a successful difficult conversation.
· Why difficult conversations are crucial for school improvement.
· The psychology behind team conflict.

You're having difficult conversations anyway

If you're reading this book it's because there are difficult conversations in your school. If you're like the school leaders I've met, you'll find difficult conversations tend to come at you, from all angles, many times a day. And let's face it, dealing with conflict is something that just happens in life; it's a leadership skill but it's also a life skill, so let's get you more skilled up in having healthy conflict.

What is the definition of a 'difficult conversation'?
A difficult conversation is a dialogue about a situation where something needs to improve (results, performance, working relationships etc.) and where voicing the issues is likely to upset someone to some degree. (If you're sure someone won't be upset then it's unlikely to be a difficult conversation.)

What is the definition of a 'successful *difficult conversation'?*
Quite simply, it is a difficult conversation that **creates positive change, quickly and kindly**.

Difficult conversation topics

The ones I've encountered the most are:

1. Not marking books frequently or well enough.

2. Poor teaching and/or poor planning.

3. Not working as a team.

4. Bullying behaviour.

5. Teaching assistant (TA) not working with a child/class well enough.

6. Year/subject leaders not driving performance across their year/subject.

7. Missing deadlines/not carrying out agreed actions.

8. Brusque receptionist.

9. Lateness.

10. Laziness.

The list is not exhaustive, and there are many more difficult conversation topics that can arise. If any of these sound familiar to you then read on, because I can help you transform these and other tricky conversations into successful ones.

Life would be easier without conflict

Life sure would be easier without conflict! Think about how many times a day you need to have a difficult conversation with a member of staff or with a parent. And that's just your professional life!

However, without conflict we cannot be as good, or great, as our potential. And when it comes to our schools and the education of our children, we all aspire to be as great as possible.

Whether you're the master of conflict or not, you're exposed to conflict every day in your role; some are big, some are small, some are petty, some are serious, but the issues can seem endless.

> **Activity 1: How many difficult conversations are you having?**
>
> Take a moment to think about how many difficult conversations have come at you and how many you need to have (whether you or not you had these conversations).
>
> How many difficult conversations have come your way this week?
> _____
>
> How many difficult conversations should you have initiated this week (whether you did or not)? ___

Successful difficult conversations help make great schools

I specialise in helping schools become great. Yes, I mean 'outstanding' but in the truest sense of educational excellence (which should get the Ofsted badge as a by-product). I've met a lot of 'outstanding' headteachers. I possibly know more than anyone else. And what I discover time and time again is that they are all concerned about getting their school culture right. How is this possible? Through three key strategies:

Figure 1: The three core leadership strategies for creating an outstanding culture

1. Create a compelling vision that inspires your team: where are we going and why should I come along?

2. Have successful difficult conversations kindly and quickly to improve staff performance and conduct issues.

3. Grow excellence in your team by developing everyone to be *excellent* in their role.

You might be thinking:

- We have a vision.
- We have difficult conversations.
- We develop and grow people through training.
- So why aren't we 'outstanding'?

It is the *quality* of each of these that makes the difference and that's something 'outstanding' heads do very well.

The one strategy that has the biggest and quickest impact is ensuring staff behaviour and performance is consistently high through mastering successful difficult conversations. You'll see the biggest return on your invested time and a big impact on making your culture higher performing because:

Culture is your team's behaviour over time.

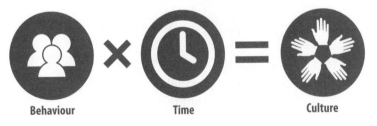

Behaviour   Time   Culture

Figure 2: The culture equation

Difficult conversations are a barrier to school improvement

Difficult situations, where things aren't as they should be, are a hidden barrier to school improvement because they drain energy from the job of education in a variety of ways:

- It might be poor teaching that isn't improving.
- It might be that mandatory paperwork has not been handed in, leaving your school leaders chasing people instead of thinking about school improvement, thus losing valuable leadership hours every week.
- It might be that someone is demonstrating bullying behaviours so that staff members are too afraid to challenge them or put forward ideas.
- It might be that a TA isn't supporting learning well enough.
- It might be a parent who doesn't want their child to be assessed in case they have a special need, which prevents you from implementing the best support for them.
- It might simply be the member of staff who wears their 'special face' (you know the one) in staff meetings and assemblies and makes others feel awkward.

I've seen all of these, and more, and in these instances you lose on at least five fronts:

Firstly, you lose because of the issue itself, such as poor quality teaching.

Secondly, you lose because someone spends time trying to improve the situation.

Thirdly, time is often spent talking about the issue; maybe in senior leadership team (SLT) meetings, or maybe through gossip around the school. This takes up your school's precious time.

Fourthly, you can lose great staff members who may get frustrated at school leaders' unwillingness to have the conversations that are needed, so you end up losing your best people and keeping the poorer performers.

Ultimately, the real loss is for the children and the quality of their education.

Imagine I waved a wand and all the difficult issues had gone away. How much time would your school get back? And how could you use that time to improve the quality of education?

Difficult conversations are feedback conversations

Feedback sits at the core of all difficult conversations and feedback is a wonderful thing. It helps us see how we can improve. Feedback is the essence of high performance. I embrace the belief that:

There's no failure, only feedback.

However, many people see feedback as criticism, as pointing out weaknesses and flaws, not as a gift to help them improve and that's why difficult conversations are so challenging. Granted, not everyone gives feedback well and the person on the receiving end can feel attacked and become defensive. However, difficult conversations should be about giving useful feedback regarding problematic performance or behaviour to help someone else. They should never be an attack on someone's character.

Shazia Akram, Outstanding Headteacher at Edward Pauling Primary School in Feltham, has feedback built into their school's improvement. Whenever they introduce a new idea or make an improvement they work hard the first time, then the team evaluate and see how they can do better and work smarter, then they evaluate again and see how they can work 'savvy'. As Shazia says:

'First, we work hard, then we work smart, then we work savvy'

This is a beautiful approach to feedback as it gives all the team permission to critique their work so they can constantly refine and improve.

School improvement is about learning to do better. Sometimes this process of improvement can work easily and people are willing to listen, but in other instances these messages are hard to deliver and hard to hear.

Elite performers understand the importance of feedback

Truly high-performing teams and organisations place a premium on the value of feedback and deliberately foster cultures that allow feedback to take place constructively, honestly and openly.

A great example of this culture in action is the aviation industry. The safety achievements of the aviation industry are legendary. Flying is statistically safer than any other form of transport, by a number of measures. This has not happened by accident; the industry has worked tirelessly to achieve, maintain and improve its safety record. Many people believe this safety record is largely down to engineering developments such as autopilots, radar or better engines (which do play a large part). What is less widely known, outside of the industry, is that one of the biggest advances in aviation safety came about through changing the culture of the entire industry via the introduction of what is most widely known as 'crew resource management' (CRM) training.

CRM can be defined as a system which utilises resources to promote safety within the workplace by improving situational awareness, communication and teamwork. CRM was introduced in the late 1970s, following analysis of several aviation disasters where the cockpit voice recorders (which record all communication in the cockpit during a flight) revealed that unclear communication in the cockpit and poor receptiveness to feedback and challenge was, in many instances, the principal reason for a tragedy. (The worst example of this is the Tenerife airport disaster in 1977, still the world's worst ever aviation disaster.)

Throughout the 1980s and 1990s CRM training became fully adopted by all the world's airlines, and captains were trained to be more receptive to feedback and challenge. All flight crew were taught to communicate critical information by clearly identifying problems and the outcome required in a manner that takes into account human emotion. Changing the behaviour of flight crews has played a huge part in making aviation safety what it is today.

As a whole, the aviation industry has established a 'no-blame' culture where feedback is welcomed and encouraged, and where every aspect of performance and behaviour is open to review and challenge. This is because they want to improve safety; a blame culture does not support that at all. This is a qualitative cultural shift because the entire industry had to change its culture by changing its behaviour.

As this example shows, the behaviours of your team are incredibly important. They create your culture because:

Behaviour breeds behaviour.

The behaviours of a group can perpetuate and form what is deemed to be 'normal' behaviour in your school context. However that 'normal' might fall short of being the best it can be.

To really understand this, we need to look at the psychology behind teams.

Tuckman's theory of group development

There are many theories and models about team dynamics, but the one I find most useful is Bruce Tuckman's (1965) theory of group development. You may or may not have heard of it, or you might know it better as 'forming, storming, norming and performing'. Let me take you through the theory, which can be seen at work as soon as you have two or more people engaged in an ongoing relationship (romantic, professional, friendship or otherwise).

Figure 3: Tuckman's (1965) theory of group development

Forming

A group or team forms, they come together and they go through a 'getting to know you' phase. Conversation is centred around friendly, factual information to build up a picture of the person or organisation; for example:

'Where do you live?'

'How many children do you have? How old are they?'

'Oh, you got married last year, so did I!'

'What are your school's top priorities this year?'

There is giving and receiving of information and people tend to be well behaved, wanting to fit in and make a good impression with the team. This is like a honeymoon period.

Storming

The honeymoon ends and storming begins. This is when the team start to test the metaphorical boundaries, and wonder:

- Is it OK to be late?
- Can I wear jeans?
- What if I don't do that piece of work on time?

People rarely test these statements explicitly or consciously, things just happen and they learn from how the team or leader reacts. They observe what others do and use that to help them understand where the lines are drawn. If someone else in the team is late to a meeting and it's OK, then it seems fair to say that I could be late to a meeting and it should be OK – it's what we can do in *this* team.

During this stage, disagreements start to appear because these boundaries are being tested and people might 'overstep the mark'. It's also a time when people might start to jostle to position themselves in the team. For example, a senior leader with many years of experience may feel that they are a more important leader in the group than the newer, younger deputy and start to position themself as such, perhaps overriding or undermining decisions or ideas given by the deputy.

It tends to be a tricky and uncomfortable time for teams and one where people often think: 'We were getting on so well and now we're not. What's gone wrong?'

Norming

Once the team has stormed they will have established some norms – hopefully good norms – with regards to how their team behaves and works. Good norms support the team to do well; bad norms hinder progress. It might be that we make sure we deliver on our agreed actions and being late is not acceptable; these are good norms. However, it might also be that a team member is likely to get upset easily and so the team treads on eggshells around them, or one team member is rude in the way that they challenge others' input. If the group is passive in cases like these – with an attitude of 'that's just the way they are' – and the rest of the team accepts this, these are bad norms.

Performing

Once the team has normed they are ready to really start performing. This doesn't mean that they haven't performed and delivered up to this point. They will have been busy, because work doesn't pause for team formation. Work is the context around which this team formation occurs but, by now, a lot of the team dynamics have been established and their energy can be focused more on their work and performance.

In a school context, you have a strong example of this theory at work.

A great example of Tuckman's theory at work is the school year

Every September, your teachers are faced with a new class of children, at this stage they <u>form</u>. During September, the class and the teacher get to know each other; generally, the children are pretty well behaved because they want to be good and impress their new teacher.

However, as we move into October and towards half term, their behaviour seems to get more challenging, as we are moving into the <u>storming</u> phase. Children are beginning to test where those metaphorical lines are. The teacher and the school will have a set of expectations for behaviour and school rules will be in place, probably the same rules the class had the previous year. But these are 'just words' and, in storming, the children will test how much these rules are adhered to, as well as testing rules that haven't been explicitly stated. So, if the teacher says 'Silent reading', a child might test if they really mean silent reading. Maybe they can whisper to the person next to them? Or maybe it's OK to draw as long as they are silent? The way a child finds out depends on the reaction of the teacher; if they are strict, then silent reading means silent reading and the teacher picks up on this when someone isn't complying, which in turn means the whole class knows silent reading really does mean silent reading. I'm sure you can think of many more examples of the unspoken class rules that children test.

The idea that children like strict teachers is a little misleading. What they actually like, as do a lot of adults, is knowing where the lines are. The lines might be tight (strict) or wide (less strict) but they should be clear and consistently applied.

Storming tends to continue through the autumn term and then December comes, when Christmas, glitter, nativities and carol singing can take over.

Returning to school in January, the class has usually settled. They know how their teacher works, they know the lines that are different in this class compared to their previous class and they are able to work within them; they have <u>normed</u>. Every now and then they will test them again and some children will find it harder to stick within those lines but, overall, the class has settled and January feels quite different from the autumn term. In fact, heads worry about a teacher who hasn't got their class behaviour in a good place by January. Alarm bells start to ring because we intuitively know that, by then, a class should have normed.

I've always thought of the spring term as the engine room of the school year. Class behaviour has settled and now the class can really get on with the job of learning. Teachers have been teaching and the children learning since September, but now it's easier and lessons flow better. The class, working like a team, can <u>perform</u> at a higher level.

Moving into the summer term, teachers are willing to do activities with their class that they wouldn't have done back in the autumn term. They can even loosen some of the boundaries, because they are well established and easier to put back in place. This is where <u>performance</u> can be notched up another level.

Does that school year sound familiar? You might also think of a time when you've had a new member join your leadership or a year group team – the same process occurs. It also happens when teams are suddenly put into a new context such as a school amalgamation, joining a multi-academy trust (MAT) or getting a new school building. The new context throws up new ways of working that teachers need to manage. So, they will need to go through this group development process again, perhaps a little faster because they already understand many aspects of their team.

One stage is more important than all others.

The importance of storming
The most important part of the Tuckman's group development cycle is storming. A group that storms well can establish constructive ways of airing issues as they arise, which means they form many good norms; this, in turn, means they have the potential to become a high-performing team. Without effective initial and ongoing storming (because issues arise as time goes by), a team will struggle to meet its full potential.

I enjoy sharing Tuckman's theory with school teams because they are quickly able to see the stage where their team is at in the process and often gain an insight around storming. Maybe the team is currently going through this rocky stage; knowing that this is a natural part of their cycle makes the rocky stage they are going through easier or, perhaps, helps them realise that they have not stormed as well as they need to.

I worked with a leadership team that ran two schools. One deputy head said to me: 'You mean it's OK to disagree? In fact, we should if there's an issue?' and my answer was 'Yes'. Disagreement needs to be conducted in the right way – as a calm discussion about issues and then working out the best solution together. This deputy went to see his head (who had decided not to attend the training days so that the team could speak more freely) and said they needed to have some healthy conflict. They sat down and aired key issues effectively and, as a result, a stronger, more effective relationship and respect developed between them. The next time I saw the deputy, he looked an inch taller and the rest of the leadership team had noticed the difference in him since his experience of effective storming. The head told me how much he was enjoying this improvement to their professional relationship and the positive impact it was having on the deputy's performance.

Storming is healthy conflict

Storming is not about arguing – it's about having healthy conflict, which is good for you and your team. Healthy conflict helps the team improve by addressing issues and giving feedback in a timely manner. Healthy conflict also makes our relationships stronger, not weaker.

Think of each conflict as being a rock. Every time an issue comes along, you get a rock to put in your rucksack. It's not going to be long before that rock begins to weigh you down.

Conversely, when we have healthy conflict we still come across issues, but this time when we get one of these 'rocks' we don't hold it for long because we have a useful discussion with the person. Instead of carrying the rocks with us, we can put it down and no longer be weighed down by it.

Dysfunctional teams

When we don't storm well, we don't have healthy conflict and so we have, to a greater or lesser degree, a dysfunctional team. I've been in high-performing and dysfunctional teams and seen both in operation; the difference is stark.

I worked with a school leadership team who had the potential to be very high performing. However, they had one member of staff who was brilliant at her job, but awful in her behaviour with the team. She was rude, openly aggressive, and sometimes passively aggressive. This meant the team walked on eggshells and cowered around her, even the head. Although she was great at her job, her behaviour was stopping the team from realising its potential. They had failed to storm well and had developed bad norms around this person. It would be easy to blame this woman's behaviour for holding the team back – which it was – but they were also contributing through their lack of storming. They needed to talk to her about their grievances, which would, of course, be hard because she was, to put it simply, a scary lady! However, she clearly cared, as otherwise she wouldn't have done her job so effectively.

Great teachers create high-performing classes

Great teachers are skilled at creating teams that develop in both their learning and their behaviour. As teachers, we are comfortable talking to children about their work, how they can improve and challenging them to do even better, but also improving their behaviour, attitude and character. We do this very easily with our classes and we do it because we want them to achieve as well they can. Feedback is an everyday occurrence in the classroom and children often handle constructive feedback better than adults!

Great leaders create high-performing teams

As leaders, we need to become comfortable and skilled at giving feedback about performance, behaviour and attitude to our adult teams. It's so much easier to have these conversations with children, something that became clear to me when I moved from the classroom to business. If we want great teams, this is a necessary skill.

When I made the move from classroom teacher to business leader, I saw my role in the team as similar to my role in class – to support a group of people to do as well as they could. Now, these were intelligent and experienced adults and I certainly wasn't their 'teacher'! We were peers working toward common goals, and my leadership approach was to support and enable which, at its core, is what we do as teachers.

This approach served me very well and, although it wasn't the reason I did it, it led to rapid promotions for my team and myself. I learnt very quickly that if I was going to support my team as much as possible, I had to get skilled at these feedback/conflict situations.

Chapter 2:
The cost of conflict

In this chapter we explore:
· How much conflict is costing you in time and money.

The business of schools is learning. In that endeavour, you have physical resources and human resources; people with skills and time. There is a limit for both, and the resource that can make the biggest positive difference is your people, their time and what they do with it.

Most of us have a funny relationship with time: we 'kill time', 'lose time' and 'waste time'. And yet, time is our most precious finite resource.

I believe we need to view time in terms of the return on time invested (ROTI). Is your team spending the precious little time they have on the tasks that matter most?

Conflict and difficult conversations are time vampires, in that they suck up valuable time from your school's 'time budget' and they obstruct time being invested in learning. And, because most of us aren't trained in how to manage successful difficult conversations, they take up far more time than necessary.

I'm sure you'd be ecstatic to be given the working hours of an extra person in your teaching team, TA team, or admin team. The chances are you've already got that extra time, it's just being used and sucked up in all the wrong places!

Activity 2: The cost of conflict

School budgets are tight, and are getting even tighter, and heads are expected to do more with less.

Conflict has many costs and the biggest cost is to your culture. Unresolved conflict also has some very real and tangible costs and there's a simple way to calculate the costs for your school.

Estimate how many <u>hours per week</u> are spent across your school on:

- Difficult conversations.
- Conflict.
- Accountability conversations.
- Gossip.
- Talking about staff performance or conduct.
- Performance improvement meetings (not your planned annual performance meetings).

Take that number and complete this sum:

_____ X 40 weeks = _____ X £25 p/hour* = _____

Hours per week   Annual time   Annual cost

* This is a weighted average hourly rate across a range of roles.

Figure 4: Cost of conflict calculation

Now you can see the cost to your school in terms of time and money. Imagine getting at least half that time back in your school – what could you do with it? Work it out as full-time equivalents (FTE) by dividing the annual time by 36 (for a 36-hour week). How many people is that? What would you say to getting that many more hours or people into your school at no additional cost?

Activity 3: Go online for an accurate cost of conflict

You can get a more accurate calculation of the cost of conflict in your school with my easy-to-fill-in spreadsheet and short video. It will take you about five minutes. Go to:

www.ukheadsup.com/resources/want-to-work-out-how-much-conflict-is-costing-your-school/

School business managers love this!

At any time of a busy day or a busy term you have limited capacity to deal with these issues, so it's important to pick the conversations that will offer the greatest benefit to your school in terms of time, money and impact.

In the next chapter, let's look at how to choose which difficult conversations should be tackled first.

Chapter 3:
Picking your battles

In this chapter, we delve into:
· Why difficult conversations are so hard.
· How to know if you should have a difficult conversation.
· Prioritising what difficult conversations are essential.
· Deciding *who* should have the conversation.
· Timing when to have the conversation.

Why are difficult conversations so hard?

Most people find these conversations nerve-racking. At the start of a training day I ask: 'Hands up if you like difficult conversations?' Of the hundreds of school leaders I've asked, only a few hands go up, with the explanation that while they don't like these conversations, they realise their value and importance and, therefore, their necessity.

So why are they so fraught with anxiety?

Activity 4: Why are difficult conversations so hard?

Take a moment to think about why you find difficult conversations so hard.

Stop, and before reading further, list at least two reasons why.

My guess is you probably included the following in your list.

The first is because we care. We know that in having a difficult conversation, we're going to say things someone else won't like hearing. Most of us don't like upsetting people and so we don't like conflict. The conversation is likely to get emotional, for them and us.

The second reason is difficult conversations with adults are quite different from difficult conversations with children. Challenging school children is easier because there is an obvious hierarchy where the class teacher is the leader of the group. As a classroom teacher, we have more knowledge and experience than children in most areas of life. However, when working with peers and superiors, speaking up can be harder. We don't always have the same position of knowledge and experience as we do as classroom teacher. The person we need to confront might be older and more experienced or may have worked at the school longer. These dynamics make the conversations harder to face. I've lost count of the number of heads who've said: 'It's easier to have these conversations with children'. And that leads us to reason three.

The third reason is because we're not trained in the art of successful confrontation. As teachers, we're taught to work with children and I've seen teachers and school leaders give feedback to children incredibly well, feedback they would struggle to give to an adult.

Many leaders have told me that they were tested in having difficult conversations in job interviews or on the National Professional Qualification for Headship (NPQH) but no one ever taught them these valuable skills. That's like testing someone's ability to teach without giving them teaching theory and skills, or asking them to take a driving test without lessons!

At no point in my Postgraduate Certificate in Education (PGCE) was I trained on how to work with the adults in the school system, my TA, colleagues or parents. In fact, when I moved from school to working at John Lewis, I couldn't understand why I could easily talk to children about their behaviour and attitude but struggled to tell a member of staff to arrive on time. (And these people were paid to come in!)

And sadly, there aren't many good role models for teaching how to handle conflict well. We might not have grown up in a family that dealt with conflict in a positive way, or we might never have worked in a team with someone who is skilled in handling conflict. If you've had a good role model, then you're very fortunate.

Difficult conversations are not capability or disciplinary conversations
I hate capability procedure. I don't think anyone really wins from it. It's hard work and is often harrowing for the head and the person going through the process. It can adversely impact on the wider team, sucking up an awful lot of time and money. I know schools that estimate spending well over £100,000 on capability and legal fees when it gets messy (and sometimes this cost is only for one issue!)

The difficult conversations we will focus on mastering are all about supporting the person to improve. In most instances they will improve, in other cases they might struggle to make the necessary changes and, if the issue is serious enough, they could find themselves in capability.

By approaching difficult conversations with the intention of helping people improve, you will be well prepared should you find yourself in capability with them. You will have done everything possible legally and, most importantly, morally. However, difficult conversations are *not* about setting ourselves up for a capability management process. You want to avoid this last resort by helping someone improve, resolving big and small existing issues and nipping new ones in the bud before they grow into major problems. Think of these conversations as starting even before informal capability.

I'm not going to help you with capability conversations. Emma Webster, Employment Solicitor and part-time tribunal judge, will walk you through these in Chapter 11.

The spectrum of difficult conversations
Difficult conversations exist on a spectrum. While none of these are 'easy' there are easier ones and harder ones.

The 'easier' difficult conversations are more straightforward, like talking to someone because they were late.

In the middle of the spectrum you usually have performance-related issues, such as not marking books, poor-quality teaching, or an ineffective TA.

At the most difficult level, we have conversations about conduct, a person's attitudes or behaviour. These could include being rude or brusque, creating a negative atmosphere, shouting at another member of staff, apathy or lack of enthusiasm – such as acting like they don't really want to be at the school. When these incidents are more than a 'one off' and form a pattern of behaviour, then they might become an issue that needs tackling. These are the conversations that people find hardest, but they are very important because they affect the culture of your school. Conduct is part of the Teachers' standards (DfE, 2011); courteous personal and professional conduct is expected as much as teaching effective lessons or marking books.

Low-level	Mid-level	High-level
Lateness	Marking	Rudeness
Clothing	Planning	Laziness
Inappropriate language	Data	Bullying

Figure 5: The spectrum of difficult conversations

Don't have every difficult conversation

I'm not going to tell you to have every difficult conversation available to you. I would be misleading you if I did and you would be miserable. We all have limited time and energy, which means we can only effectively deal with a limited number of difficult conversations at any given time. It's far better to strategically pick a few rather than try to tackle them all. Choose the ones that will have the maximum impact, ideally with the lowest level of input (time). This will give you the best return for your time invested.

Prioritising your difficult conversations

You probably have some difficult conversations that must be tackled urgently and others that are better postponed for the moment. Let's look at how you can decide which conversations to have first.

Activity 5: Who and what difficult conversations do you have?

If you have a few difficult conversations that need to be tackled (by you or your wider team) then it can be useful to jot down the cases you are aware of. These could include conversations with teachers, parents, governors, employees at the local authority, an academy or a MAT.

Who	Issue with their performance or conduct? (P or C)	What is it specifically about?	Importance rating (1 not very, 4 critical)

I realise this could be sensitive information so only write it down if you're comfortable. Otherwise, just think it through.

This activity will help you see which conversations are the most important to take on. There are a few more methods for deciding if the conversation is necessary and which ones to prioritise.

The first is the 'two-worlds' technique.

Method 1: Two-worlds technique

Is the issue important enough to *need* a conversation? This method can help you decide.

At the moment, the person is walking towards a future. It is not a completely happy one because there is an unresolved issue. Firstly, understand what the future will be if nothing changes. For example:

- They might be consistently underperforming as a teacher and heading for formal capability.
- They might create a negative atmosphere among the team and this could lead to conduct capability.
- Their class might not be making enough progress, which means they are going to be behind their peers nationally.

The negative future isn't always potential of capability, it can be to continue living with the issue which, in itself, isn't nice.

Then think about the alternative future if the issue is resolved well. This isn't simply the absence of the adverse consequences (capability, living with the issue), as it is also the positive side. The person in question will become a good teacher, they'll contribute to the team in a positive way, their class will make at least the expected progress, and the pupils and the TA will learn to be more independent.

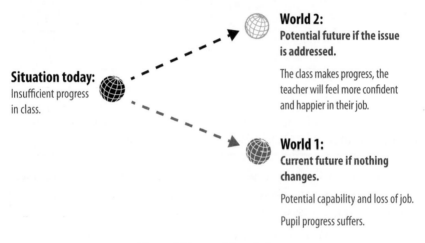

Situation today:
Insufficient progress in class.

World 2:
Potential future if the issue is addressed.

The class makes progress, the teacher will feel more confident and happier in their job.

World 1:
Current future if nothing changes.

Potential capability and loss of job.

Pupil progress suffers.

Figure 6: Two-worlds technique

The two-worlds technique allows you to see where they *are* heading and where they *could* be heading and this will tell you whether the conversation is worth the energy and time. Is there a positive enough future to work towards or not? Is the negative future bad enough that it must be avoided? This makes it a conscious and more informed choice, not reactive or avoidance.

I worked with a head that was dealing with a member of staff who was excellent in many ways, but displayed bullying behaviours. She could be an intimidating person and hard to approach; when challenged in the past, her response was extreme (shouting, storming out). The head knew he wanted to tackle this well and get the person back on track, but attempts to date had been hard work and hadn't led to any improvement. This conversation was going to be tough but, by looking at the two-worlds that lay ahead, the head found a stronger motivation to succeed, which he went on to do, using the skills I'm covering in this book. It was hard, but making the necessary behavioural changes put them firmly on the path to a brighter future, which was a real credit to them both.

Method 2: Strategically prioritising your difficult conversations
The two-worlds technique might not work for you if you've got quite a few potential conversations and you don't have the time or energy to tackle them all simultaneously. The performance/behaviour matrix in Figure 7 can help you and your team to prioritise these.

Performance		Behaviour		
	Great	3	7	9
	Good	2	5	8
	Poor	1	4	5
		Poor	Good	Great

Figure 7: Performance/behaviour matrix

This matrix helps tidy up our thinking so we can be strategic (please note: the numbers do not denote the priority for taking action – see below). There are several ways to use it. Here's how it can be used to prioritise difficult conversations and use your time and energy wisely.

1. Pick a group such as teachers, TAs or middle leaders (MLs). If there is one group that you have performance or conduct issues with, then start with them.

2. Plot them on the matrix (a large sheet of paper and sticky notes are very useful for this). Doing this as an SLT team leads to some very interesting and insightful conversations.

3. Once complete, look at where everyone is placed. This should inform you of trouble spots that urgently require difficult conversations.

There are some key sections on the matrix to consider:

Box 1
Behaviour: Poor

Performance: Poor

These are critical situations which need addressing and ones you're most likely aware of already. They tend to absorb a lot of time so consider carefully how much capacity you and your team have to manage these conversations effectively. You might need to tackle less conversations so that you can tackle these ones well.

Boxes 4 & 5
Performance is easier to improve than behaviour. It is easier to move people 'up' the performance axis than to move people 'along' the behaviour axis. So, you could focus on the low performers with 'good' or 'great' behaviours as your next group for having difficult conversations with. If I had to choose between 'good' or 'great' I would choose staff with 'great' behaviour (conduct), because they are more likely to be receptive to feedback aimed at improving their performance.

My earlier example of a head talking to a bullying member of staff impressed me so much because this person was ranked 'great' for performance but 'poor' for behaviour (Box 3) and moving horizontally along the behaviour axis can be incredibly hard, or impossible for some. The fact that the staff member found the ability to change their habitual interpersonal behaviour, and that the head was the one who started that ball rolling, is no small feat.

Activity 6: Go online to find out which is the best box to focus on

The best box on the grid to focus on is Box 8. If you'd like to know more go online to www.ukheadsup.com/performancebehaviourmatrix/

Method 3: How many times do you need to see the problem to challenge it?
The frequency of the issue is another way to decide if a difficult conversation is needed. If you've seen someone who hasn't marked their books on time once, but they usually do, you'd probably let it go. However, if you see this a second or third time, then a light-touch conversation could nip the habit in the bud.

When I was working in John Lewis I noticed that one member of my team made a point quite aggressively in a team meeting. I observed how his forcefulness affected the rest of the team and prematurely ended the discussion. I thought this was a one-off, as I'd not seen this behaviour from him before, and it was not severe enough to raise it immediately.

A few meetings later I saw the same behaviour again and spoke privately to the team member after the meeting. He wasn't aware that he'd come across aggressively and certainly did not intend to. I never saw this behaviour from him again. From then on, he would express his viewpoint and debate the subject in a cohesive way that led to lively discussion, something I complimented him on.

If you witness something serious enough, you might need to pick up on it immediately.

Be aware of your excuses
There can be good reasons for not having a difficult conversation and these three methods can help you determine if your reasons are valid. However, be wary of making excuses for avoiding the conversation. Common excuses are outlined in Figure 8.

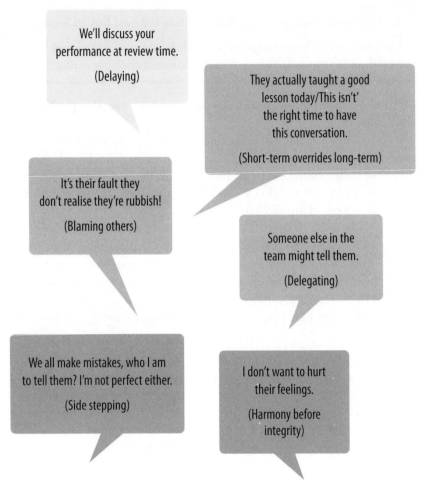

These are not good reasons to avoid the conversation.

Figure 8: Common excuses for not having a difficult conversation

Who should have the difficult conversation?

Headteachers have the majority of difficult conversations because most staff go to them about issues. However, difficult conversations should be handled as close to the source as possible; this means that they are distributed, should be addressed quickly and not be blown up into something bigger.

When it comes to difficult conversations I think of headteachers as being like the goalkeeper in a football team. In a really good team of players the goalkeeper shouldn't have anything to do, as they are last line of defence and, if the team is playing well, they shouldn't need to get involved. I think headteachers should be like this with regards to difficult conversations; the last one to get involved.

Ideally the difficult conversation should be handled by the person who has the issue that needs to be resolved. This is not always feasible and there is definitely a need for leaders to get involved with specific issues such as bullying or, at the most extreme end, cases of sexual harassment.

However, most issues don't need the head, or even a senior leader. Here are some guidelines:

Who is the difficult conversation with?	Who should typically have the conversation?
A teacher	The SLT member with line management responsibility or the phase/year group leader, if you have these
A TA	Whomever is responsible for line management
	The class teacher if it's an issue with a TA in their class
Office staff	School business manager
Parent	Class teacher as often as possible
Governor	Chair of governors
Chair of governors	Other governors or headteacher
Headteacher	Whomever has the issue*

* This is actually the answer for all.

If we're succeeding in creating a culture of healthy conflict then the head should be the last to be involved. Of course, this relies on everyone being good at handling conflict. However, we know that most people are not adept at dealing with conflict and understandably avoid it, so the issue gets passed upwards.

The schools I know that really do create a culture of healthy conflict are those that train their senior leaders, then their middle leaders and, finally, their teachers, to develop these skills. I've worked with schools where the first training day for their NQTs is on 'successful difficult conversations', because they want them to be skilled and confident in dealing with issues as they arise – both giving those messages and, also, receiving them well. Mastering these skills provides a great boost to their confidence as they start their teaching careers.

Activity 7: Who has the majority of difficult conversations?

1. Tick which statement best applies to your school:

    ☐ The head has the majority of difficult conversations.

    ☐ The SLT has most of the difficult conversations.

    ☐ Middle/phase/year group leaders have the majority of difficult conversations.

    ☐ Everyone at our school is good at having the difficult conversations they need to have and only take issues to more senior staff when necessary.

2. Put a star next to the statement you *want* to have.

If you've ticked and starred the same statement then let's have a virtual high-five!

If you've ticked and starred number four let's have a virtual high-ten!

Don't over step the mark
You're a school leader and talking about performance and conduct within the realm of school is within your remit. Be careful not to take on the position of counsellor, therapist or any other such role, even if you think that is what the person needs. If that is the person requires, then you need to direct them to the right professionals. Even if you are trained in, for example, counselling, this is not the context in which to use these skills because it is not your role in your school.

When should you have the difficult conversation?
This is a grey area and the overriding sentiment for when you have the conversation is when it is best for the other person. We want to help them improve and remove the issue, so when is the best time for them to hear and process the message? There are no perfect answers to this, but there are some guidelines.

At the time
Often, a light comment at the time of the issue can nip it in the bud. This is usually for something that has been said or done which can be picked up on immediately. For example:

> Person 1: *'It doesn't really matter if we don't get the data in on time, they won't be looking at it for a week anyway.'*

> Person 2: *'I think it does matter that we get it in on time because it's important information for us in terms of helping our students make progress.'*

When the dust has settled
Sometimes it's best to let things calm a bit before picking up the conversation, as it's too big or too heated to challenge at the time. This is a judgement call based on what you know about the person and the situation.

When you can follow up a few days later
Have the conversation at a time when you can follow up within a few days and work with the person to understand the issue and make the improvement because, while they are away, there is a danger that will make it into something bigger than it needs to be. For this reason, I would normally say don't have the conversation on a Friday, but as the example below shows this can work.

A deputy head I know had a difficult conversation with a member of staff because they were not adequately fulfilling either their leadership or teaching role. The deputy decided to have this conversation on a Friday afternoon. Normally, I would say this is a bad idea because a lot of unhelpful stewing can happen for the person and it can ruin their weekend. However, in this instance the weekend gave that person ample time to think about what had been said and to come to a conclusion about the next steps that needed to be taken themselves. When she came back in on the Monday, she had decided she wanted to leave the school and be a teacher without leadership responsibility, a decision she was visibly happy and relieved about.

So, Fridays can be a good time but, if you're not sure, I would err on the side of caution and avoid them.

As late in the day as possible

Having the difficult conversation as late in the day as possible means the person doesn't have to keep working with the conversation, and the problems raised, going through their head while they don't have the space to really think about and process it. I know this isn't always possible because you're busy, but it is a factor.

Don't save it all for your next performance management meeting

Performance management meetings are a great place to look at what someone has done well and what they can do to improve further and this might prove to be the perfect opportunity to raise an issue.

However, if there's quite some time until the next meeting, it's best to pick up the issue sooner and give someone the opportunity to improve as soon as possible.

But I don't have time for the conversation!

I know you're busy and time is precious. When I'm training school leaders, they sometimes comment that they don't have time for these tough conversations. I ask them to do the following.

Activity 8: Is it worth the extra time?

1. How many conversations have you had about this so far? _____

2. How much time have you spent on this issue so far? _____

3. (If you haven't spoken to them yet, estimate the time).

4. How effective has it been in resolving the issue, on a scale of one to ten? (1 low, 10 high) ____

Towards the end of the training I ask them:

1. How many conversations do you think you will now need to resolve this issue? _____

2. How long do you think these conversations will take if you use the skills I've taught you? ____

3. How effective do you think it will be in resolving the issue? (1 low, 10 high) _____

You can then compare the two and make an informed choice as to whether you continue as you did before or try the approaches I've given you.

If your difficult conversations are already successful then there's no need to do anything differently. If they are not then it's time to try something else. I know the following quote is overused and it's quite a cliché, but I can't think of a better way of putting it!

A definition of insanity: Keep doing the same thing and expecting a different result.

The conversation I'm training you to have is occasionally a bit longer than the conversations you are already having, but they are far more effective and so the total amount of time spent is reduced. It's about having as few conversations about the issue as possible, with each conversation being very effective.

Time	High	4) A lot of time and not much success, this is a lose/lose	2) High time but high effectiveness so it's pretty good
	Low	3) Low success but thankfully not much time	1) Bingo! This is the best – low time but high success
		Low	**High**

Success

Figure 9: Success/time matrix for difficult conversations

What format is best for the conversation?
We live in a technological world offering many mediums through which to have the conversation: text, FaceTime, email, phone, Skype and many more. There is a pecking order:

1. Face to face

2. Phone

3. Written format

We're going to look at the power of non-verbal communication in Chapter 7, because it plays a vital role in making difficult conversations successful. That's why the best way to have a conversation is face to face, because you have your full range of non-verbal communication available to you. Phone conversations are the next best method because your voice can convey a lot more than just words. The written format is the worst of the three, as it strips you of so much crucial non-verbal communication; email can often be read with an incorrect tone, which alters the way the message is received.

There is a place for the written format, usually after the conversation and certainly when you're getting into capability and disciplinary conversations. For our difficult conversations, it's the worst option even though it might sometimes be the most convenient and time effective.

There's no such thing as a perfect successful difficult conversation
I wish there was! There is a range, stretching from better to worse, and I want to help you get better at them but, no matter how well a difficult conversation goes, there will always be something you could have done better. The main gauge of success is:

1. Did it create **positive change?**

2. Did it create this change **quickly?**

3. Was the conversation **kind?**

Any exchange that could have gone better is an experience to learn from and improve upon, just like you do when teaching. Your lessons weren't all perfect, but they all helped you learn your craft, and it's the same with difficult conversations.

This applies to me as well. I can manage difficult conversations well and with a good degree of success, but it doesn't mean they are perfect. And sometimes I get them really wrong (usually because I haven't followed my own advice!)

You can learn to have successful difficult conversations
The good news is you can learn to be really good at handling difficult conversations, whether they land on you or if they are, essentially, feedback you need to give to someone. You can do this with adults, with regards to their performance and behaviour, just like you naturally do with children.

I've trained hundreds of school leaders on how to have more successful difficult conversations. The skills they have acquired have a positive impact on their school and their own ability to lead. At the time of writing, every school leader who has been trained would recommend our training. It's this training that I will be sharing with you in the next section of this book.

I'm going to cover a lot in this next section. To help you use it to improve your difficult conversations I've included my checklist for successful difficult conversations in Appendix D. Using this will ensure you're covering all the bases before, during and after a difficult conversation.

Section 2

How to have successful difficult conversations

Chapter 4: The three core components of a successful difficult conversation

In this chapter, we discuss:
· The three common problems with difficult conversations.
· The three core components of successful difficult conversations.

I've witnessed a *lot* of difficult conversations – thankfully not all my own – and there are three common problems I see repeatedly, no matter what the topic. Maybe you've also experienced some, or all, of these.

The three common problems in difficult conversations

Problem 1: The person doesn't hear your message

You raise an issue with someone, you're as clear as you can be, you give your message in several different ways but, when they walk away, you feel like they didn't hear what you were telling them. In fact, you might feel they've heard something else. It's frustrating and can you make you feel like it wasn't worth having the conversation in the first place.

Problem 2: It gets emotional

When we're giving a message that is hard for someone to hear, emotions can increase; they may cry, withdraw or get angry. This can be hard on us as well as them, because we didn't give them the message to cause distress; we gave it to help them to improve. But we're human and we can react emotionally.

Emotions come into play before, during and after the conversation. Have you ever worried about a conversation you knew you needed to have? Perhaps you've played it over in your mind or it's become the low point in your week ahead. After the conversation, have you ever replayed it, relived or even reinvented it, imagining what you could have said and then how they would have responded, even though the conversation is over? If so, you're not alone.

The problem with these emotions is that they can be exhausting and use up a lot of your energy, which means there's less energy for the rest of school and your home life.

A memorable example of the impact that emotions can have was with a school leader that I trained. As we started the day, she told me how she had a difficult issue with a person in her school and that she took this woman on holiday with her. She was by the pool with her, at dinner with her and on the beach with her. I thought 'Why would you take this person on holiday with you?', and then I realised; she wasn't physically with her, she was in her head throughout the holiday. This school leader was reliving, replaying and reinventing the conversation she'd had with her colleague, and it was ruining her holiday!

Problem 3: No change happens
You know this situation: you have a difficult conversation with someone, they agree with what you say, including what they need to do next. But you're pretty sure none of the changes will actually happen which means that, despite putting yourself through a difficult conversation, sadly, you might as well have not bothered!

A senior leader I worked with had exactly this problem. For a year he'd been repeatedly asking a capable team member to complete some necessary paperwork. However, for an entire year, the paperwork had not materialised. We worked on the three core components and, after the next conversation, this previously uncooperative staff member produced all the paperwork within eight hours.

Activity 9: What is the biggest problem for you?

Think of up to five recent difficult conversations you've had that didn't go well and enter them in the table below. Tick the problems you experienced.

Conversation	1. Didn't hear my message	2. It got emotional	3. Didn't make changes	Other
1				
2				
3				
4				
5				

Circle the most common problem in your difficult conversations.

The three core components of successful difficult conversations

There are three core components that, when all in place, will dramatically increase the success of your difficult conversations, no matter what the topic. They tackle the three common problems head on.

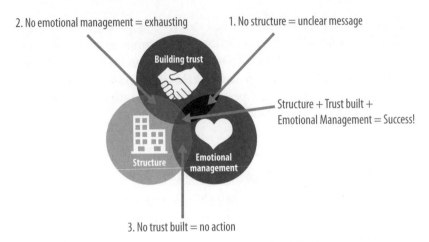

2. No emotional management = exhausting   1. No structure = unclear message

Building trust

Structure + Trust built +
Emotional Management = Success!

Structure   Emotional management

3. No trust built = no action

Figure 10: The three core components of successful difficult conversations

Core component 1: Structure – make sure your message is heard

When someone doesn't hear your message it's usually because your message is unclear. I know you might feel that you have been crystal clear, but I've seen hundreds of school leaders who believe they have a clear message when they do not. In fact, it is the single biggest mistake I see in around 70% of difficult conversations. It's a tricky problem to fix, but one I will help you with.

Core component 2: Emotional management – stops the conversation being exhausting

Emotions are exhausting and can derail a successful difficult conversation, as well as make them occupy too much of our thoughts before and after a conversation. They are, however, an important and inevitable part of these conversations, so learning how to manage our own and the other person's emotions is crucial.

Core component 3: Trust – increases the likelihood of positive action

When the other person doesn't take action from the conversation, whether they said all the right things or not, is due to a lack of trust. I'm not talking about trust that you might have built from knowing someone for a decade, or having grown up with them. I'm referring to the trust in the interaction itself. Often, we inadvertently sabotage trust through our non-verbal communication and this reduces the effectiveness of our conversation.

Understanding the core components of difficult conversations

One of the key shifts for a team, such as the SLT, middle leadership team (MLT) or year group leaders, is that when they understand these three components of successful difficult conversations they can reflect and analyse the interaction more effectively, because they have a framework and language for difficult conversations. Without this knowledge, the analysis of a conversation tends to be unhelpful and take the form of 'I said' or 'He/she said' or 'Perhaps if you'd said', and this doesn't enable you to have more effective conversations. With this knowledge, teams are better able to support one another with their difficult conversations.

To draw a parallel, this is akin to what you can do when you've observed a lesson where you know what was or wasn't working and can explain this clearly. This is the level teams get to once they understand the mechanisms at work in a difficult conversation.

In this section I'm going to tell you how you can put each of these three components in place and increase the success of your difficult conversations. I will break the core component of structure down over two chapters. The first chapter will look at getting your message across clearly and the second will be about structuring the whole conversation. The former is such a big problem that I want to devote a chapter to clarity of message to help you crack this tough nut. We'll spend a chapter on emotional management and another on building trust in the interaction.

Chapter 5: Getting the conversation started

In this chapter, we learn:
· The most common mistake made during difficult
  conversations and how to crack it.
· The only black-and-white rule of difficult conversations.
· **How to successfully start a conversation for success.**

'Starting the conversation' falls under the core component of 'structuring the conversation', covered in Chapter 8. However, I've chosen to single out this key skill with an entire chapter because getting off to a faulty start is a very common mistake that is hard to recover from, like stumbling off the starting blocks! By honing your 'starting skill', we can ensure you take off smoothly.

What happens if we start the conversation badly?
There can be several consequences to a faulty start.

- The person walks away not having heard the message you wanted to give them.
- You find yourself talking about another topic with the person.
- The conversation gets pulled off track into lots of other 'things'.
- You find that you have a list of things to do from your meeting and the other person has little or nothing to do (even though the

meeting was about addressing an issue around something they are or not doing).

Activity 10: What issues do you experience because of the start of your conversation?

Do any of these outcomes sound familiar to you? Highlight the ones you have experienced. Put a star next to the one you have experienced the most.

Most of the time when the other person walks away not having heard the message you wanted to convey, it's usually because *you* haven't been clear enough, not because *they* haven't listened.

Why is starting so hard?
A smooth start is hard because it's a multi-faceted problem.

Firstly, finding the words to start the conversation can be hard. Actually saying them to the person can be even harder!

Secondly, it can be tough to figure out what the conversation is actually about, or the real issue.

I'm going to help you with both of these challenges.

How to start the conversation
'But how do you start the conversation?' is a question I'm asked constantly during training days. People find initiating the discussion quite stressful and I understand why. We're going to tell someone something they probably don't want to hear and, even though we're raising the issue to help them, we know they are likely to have a negative emotional response. Most of us don't want to upset someone, because we care.

The opening of your difficult conversations is the only part I advise you to prepare for, to the point of having a script. There are several ways to open and I want to give you the most reliable one:

I, issue, the outcome

The commas demarcate the three sections of the sentence.

Start with 'I'

Start by saying something like: 'I feel', 'I think', 'I've been told', 'I've observed', 'I've noticed', 'I've heard'. Find the words that work for you.

Starting with 'I' is softer and less accusatory than starting with 'you'.

This opener lets you put across what you are thinking or feeling; you're not stating it as fact, you're saying this is what you believe to be the case and indicating there is room for reconsideration if you're wrong. You are simply sharing your perspective.

The issue

Next, you state the issue that has led you to have the conversation.

The outcome

Lastly, you state what you want the outcome to be, outlining the end result of the positive change you're hoping to achieve with this person.

The mistake within the mistake

When I train school leaders I'll see them start with 'I' and then say what the issue is. However, where they fall down, time and time again, is by failing to assert the desired outcome.

In Stephen Covey's popular book *The 7 Habits of Highly Effective People* (2004), the second habit he talks about is to:

'begin with the end in mind.'

This is 'the outcome' that should be present in your opening sentence.

School leaders often leave out the desired outcome because it can seem so obvious:

- I'm talking to you about being late – so surely it's clear I want you to be on time?

- I'm talking to you about the lack of quality marking in your books – so surely you know what I want is better marking in your books?

- I'm talking to you about looking disinterested in staff meetings – so surely you know I want you to be interested and engaged in staff meetings?

Maybe the other person does know what you want and you don't need to say it. However, by articulating a clear outcome, even if it seems obvious, you can dramatically increase the chance of success and reduce the need for another conversation.

If you don't say the outcome, you will find yourself in the 'swamp of issues'. This is where your conversation is all around the issue and doesn't move onto the change you need to see.

This three-part opening sentence is your guiding star in a difficult conversation and will really help you keep on track and on topic.

Let's see what an opening sentence looks like across the spectrum of difficult conversations.

Low-level difficult conversations (punctuality):
'I notice you have been late four times over the last two weeks and the school needs you to be ready to work at 8:30am every day.'

Mid-level difficult conversations (performance issues):
'I've seen from your data that your class are not making the expected level of progress and I need you to find a way to ensure that they all make at least the expected progress by the end of the school year.'

High-level difficult conversations (staff conduct):
'I feel you can come across as rude to parents at times and I would like you to express yourself in a positive manner throughout the school day, especially towards parents.'

You can amend the wording to suit your personal style, and there are nuances as to how you word your opening sentence, but I hope you can see the three elements of 'I, issue, the outcome' at play. If you cut 'the outcome' from these sentences it reduces the clarity of what you require from the other person.

Ideally, a difficult conversation should be a 'one-hit wonder' and properly resolve the crux of the issue in one go. I want you to have as few difficult conversations as possible, so if you can resolve an issue in one or two conversations, that's better for all involved. Including a specific outcome makes success more likely because it reduces the margin of error in terms of the other person guessing what they are meant to do. They will know exactly what you want them to do. However, you will always need to have a follow-up conversation, which shouldn't be as difficult and, ideally, it will be a positive one. I'll cover follow up in Chapter 8.

There are a few extra pieces of information you need to complete this opening sentence.

The only black-and-white rule in successful difficult conversations

Most of what we are doing in difficult conversations resides in the land of 'grey', non-hard and fast rules; but there is one black-and-white rule:

> *If you don't have evidence to back up the issue, do not have the conversation until you do.*

Failing to do this is like walking into a court of law without any evidence to back up the crime you're accusing someone of committing.

I have observed many conversations where the issue has been stated and the person asks for evidence: 'When did I do that?' or 'When didn't I do that?' Meanwhile, the school leader has sat there unable to recall any specific incidents, even though they know there have been plenty. We can avert this awkward scenario by going into the conversation with specific evidence.

For straightforward issues, such as lateness – how often and when? The more specific you can be the better, so having dates and times is preferable.

For performance issues, such as not marking books – what was wrong with the marking? Was it in all subjects? Wasn't it regular enough? Was the feedback not good enough? How long has this been the case?

For conduct issues – what is the behaviour that leads you to think that someone is lazy or rude? You need to be able to give very specific examples. For these issues, evidence can be harder to find because examples can be tricky to pinpoint, but they are there. Examples might include: 'In staff meetings you appear to be texting on your phone' or 'Your responses can be abrupt, like last Tuesday when you spoke to....' Just because these behaviours don't seem to be hard facts, such as lateness, it doesn't mean they are not valid.

You only need to use this evidence if someone challenges the points you raise, either by asking how you know, or by denying the issue exists. At this point, you bring out your evidence. If they accept the issue you don't need to bring forward your examples unless it's to provide clarity. For example: 'Your marking isn't at the quality level we need, because it doesn't tell students what their next steps are.'

Prepare your opening sentence
As I said earlier, this is the only part of the conversation you can prepare and my advice is that you do this carefully. You now know the sentence structure and the type of examples you need if it becomes necessary to back up your claim with evidence. I have watched many school leaders try to have a difficult conversation without preparing their opening sentence and it leads to a failed conversation.

I know how powerful a clear start is. Even if I need to have a difficult conversation with my husband I write down my opening sentence. Yes, you read that correctly. He knows I do this. And the reason is that if I'm not going to do this for him, one of the most precious people and relationships I have in my life, I'm not going to do it for anyone. I want these difficult conversations to go well, and so five minutes of preparation is well worth it.

When you do write down your sentence, understand that it will probably take you four or five attempts to get it right.

1. Typically, your first opening statement is quite long, it might be a couple of sentences.

2. The second is shorter but still not as clear as it could be.

3. The third version is shorter and clearer.

4. The fourth, or sometimes fifth, is clear, concise and caring. Bingo!

Tips and traps for your opening
Here are some tips to improve your opening and some traps to watch out for.

Numbering
Numbering is great if there are few things that need to be addressed. This

might be done at a macro (whole-school) level (e.g. overall poor teaching) or within an issue itself (e.g. aspect of marking).

At a macro level, it might be that someone's teaching is sub-standard and we might say:

'I've observed that your teaching has been less than good for half a term now and we need your teaching to be consistently good.'

There might be some specific points you could highlight to help the other person understand the issue. If their teaching isn't good then there will be reasons why, such as pace, behaviour issues, or because the activities aren't well pitched. We can bring these specifics into the conversation:

'I've observed that your teaching requires improvement for half a term now and we need your teaching to be consistently good.

Specifically, there are two issues:

The first issue is that the activities are not pitched at the right level for your class.

The second issue is that the pace of the lessons is often too slow and the children lose interest.'

Using numbers is great because they let someone know how long the list is, which means they know when the end of the list is near. If we simply start saying the list, it can feel overwhelming to the listener and hinder their ability to hear us because they start to feel emotional about the fact that there seems to be a lot of problems being raised.

Foggy words
Avoid 'foggy' words such as 'improve' or 'better'.

A deputy head needed a member of her team 'to lead better'. This is really hard for someone to act on clearly: how many ways can you think of to 'lead better'? When we got down to the nub of the issue what was needed was for the year leader to plan better with her team, as well as submitting her own plans on time. This was far more specific and avoided foggy words, and it meant that the year leader had a real chance of making the improvements because they were so clear.

When you review your sentence, look out for these foggy words and make them clearer.

Simple language

Use simple language and, by this, I'm referring to words with no more than three syllables. In fact the fewer syllables, the better. This has nothing to do with the intellectual capacity of the person you're talking to; it's because lots of long words are hypnotic and make it hard to take in a message. If you're interested, there is a calculation for fog factor (how readable a piece of text is) that you can find online (this is the Gunning Fog Index (1944) readability scoring formula, search for 'fog factor' and it will pop up). For our purposes, when you review your sentence see if you can make the language simpler and avoid words with three syllables or more, wherever possible.

Check your sentence with someone

Your sentence should be so clear that a trusted colleague is able to see what you are trying to achieve without having a conversation about it. So, ask someone you trust (and has read this book) to check your opening sentence and suggest ways to improve it.

Change the outcome

Most of the time your outcome will be right; however, if through the course of the conversation you think it needs changing, then change it. Sometimes we can get locked into the outcome, but you can be flexible where appropriate so you are working towards the right outcome and the ideal outcome.

Don't give them the sandwich

Have you heard of 'the sandwich'? This is a technique for giving feedback or delivering a difficult message. The formula is to sandwich a criticism between two compliments: open with something good, then say something 'constructive', then end with something good.

Please feel free to disagree with me on this point, but I don't like the sandwich when it comes to difficult conversations and I will elaborate on why in Chapter 12.

Activity 11: Your opening sentence

Think of a difficult conversation you need to have and write down your opening sentence the first time. Now apply tips and look out for the traps above and improve it. Try to improve your sentence at least four times.

Having the real conversation

To recap, I said that there are two main reasons why starting the conversation is hard. We have looked at finding words to get the conversation off to a good start.

The second challenge is more difficult. It's about making sure you're having the 'real conversation' that needs to be had and, to help you avoid getting derailed, there are two traps I'd like to share with you. I call them 'sirens' (like those in Greek mythology) because I think they are traps that we are seduced into falling in.

Solution siren

This is where we focus on what the *solution* is instead of the *outcome*, which means you're talking about the wrong thing and won't bring about the desired change.

Low-level difficult conversations (punctuality):
'I notice you have been late four times over the last two weeks, so you need to set your alarm earlier.'

Mid-level difficult conversations (performance issues):
'I've seen from your data that your class is not making the expected level of progress, so you need to do x, y and z.'

High-level difficult conversations (staff conduct):
'I feel you can come across as rude at times. I know it can be hard at the end of a long day, this is what I do to help me manage my mood...'

I'm not saying you shouldn't give advice, but this opening sentence is neither the time nor place for it. In giving the solution, we are implying that we know what has caused the problem. You might be right, you might not, and so the solution you suggest might not be the best one for that person. You risk having a whole conversation about the wrong thing. By focusing on the outcome at the outset, and not what might solve the problem, you are far more likely to get the result you want. Remember you want to 'begin with the end in mind'; the solution is not the end, it's the *method* and it's too early in the process for that discussion.

Symptom siren

This point is interesting and helps us understand when we're not having the real conversation that needs to be had.

It happens when we are looking at a few issues – perhaps a teacher's behaviour management isn't as good as it can be, they don't submit their data on time, their plans don't seem well thought out, or maybe their attire is scruffy and unprofessional. When the symptom siren is calling we try to fix each of these, perhaps with some very good use of numbering to structure the conversation. But many issues suggest there is a bigger problem that really needs to be addressed. When you find yourself in this kind of situation, try to take a step back and see if these issues are symptoms of a different problem and ask yourself if that's the real conversation you need to have.

I supported a head who needed to have a difficult conversation with a teacher about several issues regarding classroom behaviour and the quality of their teaching. As we talked, the head said that they felt that the teacher didn't want to be at the school anymore. This was the core issue that needed to be raised and the other issues were the evidence that gave that impression. The head had this conversation and it went well, moving everything forward more quickly than if he had tackled the issues separately one at a time. He was having the real conversation that needed to be had.

Chapter 6: Managing the emotions of difficult conversations

In this chapter, we learn about:
· What is happening emotionally during difficult conversations.
· Changing the other person's behaviour.
· Reducing the emotional energy of difficult conversations.

Emotional management is the second core component of successful difficult conversations. It's hard to have a difficult conversation without it becoming emotional. This typically happens during the conversation, but our emotions can come into play before and after too. Beforehand we can dread, agonise or rehearse the conversation and afterwards we can stew on the exchange, reliving or reinventing what happened.

This emotional energy can be very draining and, as we looked at earlier, this takes away time and energy from the work you really want to do to improve your school.

How to change the other person's behaviour
You can't change someone else's behaviour. But you can change your own. And this secret is what lies at the heart of this chapter. By being in greater control of our own behaviour we can have a positive impact on the other person's actions. I've seen this repeatedly. Our interactions are

like tennis games, one person does something, the other responds and the ball is hit back and forth. But if we can take greater control of how we respond, then we can change the course of the interaction; just as the greatest tennis players are the best at responding to what is thrown at them and have the power to change the course of a game.

Managing our emotions during a difficult conversation

To help us understand emotions and how to manage them, I'd like to turn to psychiatrist Eric Berne (1964) and his theory of transactional analysis (TA). I love this theory because it is beautifully simple and easy to use. When I studied TA at university, I was told it would explain every relationship in my life. I thought this was a bold claim, but it turned out to be true.

I'm going to give an overview of this theory. TA theory has continually developed over the past 50 years and, if you're interested, you can study it in greater depth.

The theory proposes that people move between three broad ego states:

1. Parent (P)

2. Adult (A)

3. Child (C)

Both Parent and Child have several states within them, let's look at each of these in turn.

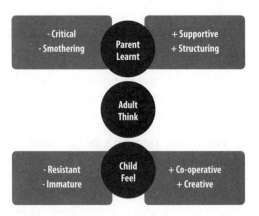

Figure 11: A summary of the Parent, Adult and Child in transactional analysis

Parent

The Parent ego state of the psyche contains the beliefs, admonitions, feelings and behaviours of parent figures accumulated during our formative years. These are the rules, opinions and actions we absorb and role model growing up and they stay in the psyche throughout one's life. When we feel threatened we can become defensive and call on the critical parent mode to judge, criticise, complain and lecture. We often hear ourselves sounding just like our mum or dad or other parent figures.

You will see in Figure 12 that there are four modes of the Parent ego state, some positive and some negative.

Negative parent roles	Positive parent roles
The critical parent	**The supportive parent**
Judgemental	Caring
Authoritative	Nurturing
Telling others off	Considerate
Patronising	
Knows best	
The smothering parent	**The structuring parent**
Overprotective	Caring but firm
Spoiling	Offers constructive criticism
Interfering	Helps to set boundaries
Suffocating	Helps to organise

Figure 12: The four versions of the parent role

Child

In Berne's model, the Child ego state is the part of the psyche developed in childhood (and throughout life) to follow the rules in order to get accepted, loved and cared for.

The positive Child is co-operative and eager to please while the negative Child can be rebellious and resistant. The TA model has been further developed to recognise a creative child with positive traits, such as being creative, fun-loving and spontaneous, and negative aspects, such as being wild and irresponsible, in the immature child. The Child part of the psyche stays with us throughout life and we can easily regress into this state in certain situations and relationships.

As we grow up we can still display childlike behaviours. I'm sure we've all wished another adult would 'grow up' and, at times, we see ourselves behaving in childlike ways. This ego state can be driven by strong emotions.

Negative child roles	Positive child roles
Resistant	**Co-operative**
Oppositional	Seeks to please
Stubborn	Wants to help
Obstinate	Wants validation
Immature	**Creative**
Doesn't take responsibility	Fun
See things as 'not fair'	Spontaneous
Can be reckless	Likes to play
Impulsive	Energetic

Figure 13: The four versions of the child role

Adult

The Adult ego state functions in the here and now with rational thinking, emotions and behaviour. In this state, we are in control of our feelings and are aware when feelings are not backed by evidence. I'm sure you have relationships that are Adult, typically these are the people who give you the best advice and clarity. They help you see things clearly and untangle your thinking.

The adult role is evidence-based, rational, not threatening or threatened. It uses:

- Open questions.
- Comparative expressions.
- Evidence.
- Objective understanding of reality.
- Reasoned statements: true, false, probably, possibly, I think/realise/believe, in my opinion.

There are times and places for all of these roles depending on the situation. The skill is picking the right one for the right time.

In difficult conversations, we want to be in the Adult role.
I find the Adult role fascinating, so much so that I began to be more conscious of using it when talking to children, especially when they were upset or angry. By being a warm adult, instead of a parent in my response, they would work through their emotions more effectively.

Activity 12: Watch TV

Pick a show you enjoy and next time you watch it, see if you can work out which of Berne's ego states the characters are in.

The games people play
Berne aptly titled his book *Games People Play*. He noticed that people play games in these roles, that each interaction is a transaction; some are complementary, some are not.

Complementary transactions are where the transactions don't cross like in Figure 14. Uncrossed transactions are where there is a cross over like in Figure 15. See overleaf.

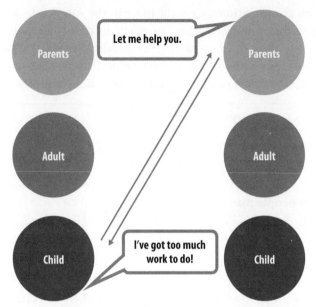

Figure 14: Complementary transactions

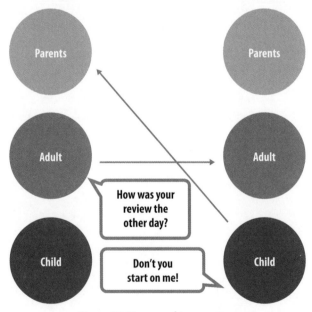

Figure 15: Uncrossed transactions

Uncrossed transactions can feel awkward. In difficult conversations, when you are trying to be in the Adult state, you might find yourself in an uncrossed transaction, which can feel uncomfortable. As a result, you might feel the pull towards being in a more complementary role; for example, in Figure 15 that might be to become either a Parent or a Child. Another example might be:

Person 1 (adult): How was your review the other day

Person 2 (child): Don't you start on me!

Person 1 could reply from any of these different ego states, for example:

Co-operative child: Oh no! I'm so sorry, are you OK?

Resistant child: Don't start having a go at me, I was only asking!

Smothering adult: Oh you poor thing, let me make you a cup of tea.

Critical parent: How dare you talk to me like that. Who do you think you are?

However, this isn't going to help you resolve the issue any better and could just perpetuate it. The reason some of your difficult conversations are not resolving could be because there is a game at play, one that isn't useful. The Adult response would be:

'I'm sorry you seem to have had a hard day. What would help right now?'

This will move the other person toward a more adult state and change their behaviour. School leaders ask me 'what if the other person doesn't move to adult?' If *you* are truly being adult they will move in the vast majority of instances. It might take a few more adult responses from you, but stick with it and the other person will shift ego states most of the time.

The first step is to recognise the roles at play, especially the role you find yourself being drawn into. The next step is to consciously adopt the Adult ego state.

A special educational needs co-ordinator (SENCO) I trained told me that she now understood why her conversations weren't successful; she was going into a child role and the whole interaction descended into an unsuccessful conversation. While she is still working at being the adult in these specific situations, at least now she understands what is going on and can work to improve, whereas previously she was not aware.

Being adult

It can be hard to adopt the Adult state, especially in difficult conversations when the other person is in a Parent or Child state and can really press your buttons. Here are some tips that will help you.

1. 'Adult' is like being a friendly scientist

You are curious and interested, observing and analysing the evidence. We are often like this with children in our schools; however, it can just feel harder with adults. Look for the evidence and treat the problem almost like an experiment on a table, complete with Bunsen burners and conical flasks. It's your job to figure out what is going on.

2. Share your emotions

If you feel you're creeping into Critical Parent or another role and that you're getting annoyed you can share this, in an adult way, by saying: 'I can feel I'm getting annoyed because I think we're going around in circles.' Keeping an adult tone of voice is crucial in making a sentence like this effective.

3. Tone of voice

The different roles are most evident in tone of voice, so be clear in your own mind what your Adult tone of voice sounds like. Be careful not to confuse this with a Parent voice because often we think of the two as being one and the same.

4. Slow the conversation down

Take some time to pause and think. In slowing the pace down you will find it easier to stay in or move back into Adult.

5. Breathing is a big easy step

When we're stressed or anxious our breathing can become faster and shallower. Before heading into a difficult conversation take three very slow breaths: slow as you breathe in and slow as you breathe out. Give your brain the oxygen it needs and, by changing your physicality in this way, you tell your body that you are calm.

All roles have a place

I'm not saying you should never be in Parent or Child roles; they all have a place in our lives. When my niece falls over and bangs her knee she doesn't get an Adult response from me such as 'I notice you have fallen over, how might you avoid that in future?' She gets a smothering parent: 'Oh my darling, come here, it's OK. I know it hurts, shhhh' and many hugs and kisses. There's great joy in being in Creative Child and playing and at times you, like me, might have needed someone to be the Critical Parent for you or to be that person for someone else. We're human, we have emotions and there's a time and place for the full range.

In difficult conversations the Adult ego state will serve you best because we want to make work about work and not about drama.

The drama triangle

One of the best-known transactions from Berne's theory is the drama triangle (Figure 16). The dynamics are well known because so much of our storytelling is based on this behaviour:

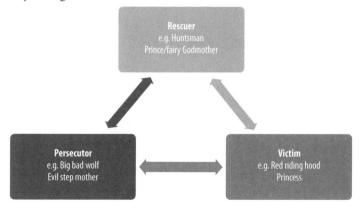

Figure 16: The drama triangle

In the drama triangle there is a Rescuer, a Persecutor and a Victim. I've seen this model at play in schools. Let's take the example of a difficult conversation where we are trying to improve a teacher's quality of teaching. In this example:

- The head or a senior leader is the **Persecutor**.
- The teacher is the **Victim**.
- The union representative is the **Rescuer**.

However, you can take the same situation and view it differently:

- The head or a senior leader is the **Victim** (because the teacher won't improve).
- The teacher is the **Persecutor** (because they are going out of their way to be difficult).
- A legal adviser is the **Rescuer** (helping the head work through this situation).

This is drama being played out, with the narrative sitting over the interactions. By being Adult, we want to move away from drama and get back to factual information:

- A teacher's teaching isn't at the required level.
- What can be done to improve their teaching as quickly as possible?

Be aware of these games, they form easily because we are very familiar with these narratives.

Activity 13: What games are you playing?

Think about some of the difficult conversations you've had. What roles did you and the other people take on? Is there one role you find yourself in more often than others?

On learning about the ego states an assistant head at a large secondary school realised he would slip into Co-operative Child when having accountability conversations with staff. He was nice and pleasant and helpful with everyone, but his approach was not leading to positive change because he was aiming to please in difficult conversations and this was shown by him taking on a lot of actions himself that would help the other person improve. This took ownership of the issue away from the team and made his difficult conversations ineffective. As he adjusted his style to Adult, his conversations became more effective, while still being kind.

Managing *our* emotions before and after the conversation

Difficult conversations create emotions in us *before*, *during* and *after* the conversation, so it is important for us to look at the *before* and *after* as well.

Become a superhero

Our bodies and brains are feedback loops so be aware of what your body is telling your brain and try to manage the feelings. Amy Cuddy (2012) provides insight into how you can put yourself into a better place mentally by being aware of what you do physically. Her research shows that:

Our bodies change our minds.

Our minds change our behaviour.

Our behaviour changes our outcomes.

She talks about how to counteract feeling nervous by adopting a power pose, like the Wonder Woman/Superman pose: stand with your legs astride and your hands on your hips and hold it for at least two minutes. This releases testosterone, which makes you feel confident, and lowers cortisol, which makes you feel stressed. If you're feeling nervous before a difficult conversation, or any other event, then try this out.

Reframing

We can manage our emotions using a technique called reframing which puts us in touch with our Adult state. If you are ruminating on a conversation, the voice in your head is the Parent or Child and it's amazing how long these voices can keep talking. In the same way that a painting can look very different in a new frame, when we reframe our thoughts we're trying to see the situation in a new way; the positive frame comes from our adult voice. Find a sentence that is your adult's perspective on the situation. You might need to try this a few times before you find one that works and you'll know when you have found the right sentence because the emotions will subside. If they rise again, which they can because that Parent or Child is still in there badgering you, the sentence should work to quieten that voice. If it doesn't, then it's not a powerful enough Adult reframe and you need to find another sentence.

A head once gave me a wonderful example of a reframe. He was meeting with some parents about their son who had very challenging social behaviour, which affected his class. The issues had persisted for some time and the head was getting exasperated because the parents were not making the agreed actions to help change things for the boy so that he could improve his behaviour at school, get on better with his peers and learn. Berne's 'critical parent' was speaking loudly in his head: 'Why can't they just get on with?'; 'I can't believe I'm having to speak about this again!.' And then he thought to himself: 'There's a seven-year-old boy at the centre of this who needs the adults around him to get it right.' Boom! He had a powerful, responsible Adult reframe which allowed him to go into the meeting and do what needed to be done without taking in any unhelpful transactional analysis roles.

We're human and, as such, we're going to move between these different states. There's nothing wrong with that; in fact, I think it's right that we do. In difficult conversations we want to be Adult and reframing helps you do this by managing your emotions before and after the conversation.

Managing *their* emotions after a difficult conversation

If the conversation has been an emotional one, especially for the other person, touch base with them within the next few days to see how they are feeling and discuss their thoughts since the conversation. Treat this as an opportunity to show them you care and hear any concerns that might have come up. Successful difficult conversations are about a dialogue.

86

We've all been in those frustrating situations after the exchange when we've thought of points we wanted to make or questions we wanted to ask, if only we'd remembered at the time. So, give them that opportunity as it might help you make further progress with the issue.

Common questions about emotions

There are questions I am frequently asked about handling emotions that I will cover in case you have the same concerns. There are no hard and fast rules as to how you respond to these volatile scenarios and my advice needs to be taken within the context and knowledge you have about the person and the situation.

What do I do if they cry?

Short answer: let them cry. Stop talking to give them space, kindly pass them some tissues, maybe offer to get them some water.

There are many reasons someone might cry during a difficult conversation and I do think, in the vast majority of instances, the tears are genuine.

Crying can be a release

It might be that you're having a conversation that is long overdue and loaded with a build-up of stress and pressure. Perhaps the problem has been a burden for the person, and crying is the first important step to acknowledging the issue and allowing their inner struggle to surface, before moving forward to solve the problem.

Crying because we can't help it

Sometimes a person can't help but cry, perhaps because what you have raised has hit a raw nerve and triggered an emotional release. Sometimes crying is just what happens. Their natural response is not your fault – you have not been unreasonable, unkind or cruel and you do need to raise the issue, despite how hard it can be for you both.

Crying because we've learnt the conversation stops when we do

I'm not saying this is a deliberate, conscious diversion by the person who resorts to crying. The instant tears could just be a response they have learned, because when they have cried in previous situations the conversation has stopped. Resist the impulse to end the conversation when someone cries for two reasons.

1. You don't want to convey the idea that crying works as a 'tactic' for ending the uncomfortable conversation, at least not with you.

2. Crying indicates there could be some hidden, painful problems with the issue raised and the emotional release could be a real breakthrough. Ending the talk because of tears might actually be uncaring and dismissive of their distress. Suddenly breaking the connection denies you both the chance to explore the deeper issues and have a valuable conversation.

As mentioned earlier you need to be careful not to step into roles beyond your remit. Tears don't automatically mean you are in that territory.

I know it can be uncomfortable but try to be OK with crying. I don't mean you should be coldly indifferent, but accept tears as something that happens. Convey the soothing message that: 'It's OK and we can work through this'. Often, crying can be the best release for a person and allows you to help them (without being a 'smothering parent').

However, if they become extremely upset you might feel it's appropriate to offer to postpone the meeting. Only do this once you've sat and held the space for a while, for the reasons I've outlined above, because you want to be sure it's not possible to continue the conversation here and now. If you do offer to postpone the meeting, arrange a date and time but, if they are too fragile, give them a time frame such as 'before the end of the week/by this time next week'. I've purposely said 'offer' to move the meeting because you should let them choose: continue now or have it within the suggested time frame. In most instances, they will know what's best for them and, by asking them to make the decision, you will move them into the Adult state.

What if they get violent?

In very rare cases, people can become angry when confronted and shout verbal abuse, bang fists or throw things! This aggressive behaviour could escalate to threatening you physically. As with crying, this could be a lifetime habit for handling a perceived 'attack'. Such an outburst can be intimidating. If this happens, it is essential to make yourself safe. If you suspect a conversation could get violent take steps beforehand to protect yourself. Your safety and the safety of those around you must always come first. Such an unacceptable outburst requires following up with a warning or taking the step of disciplinary action.

What if they walk out?

Some people automatically flee from conflict. They run away like a frightened child or flounce off with a flourish in a childish huff! Let them walk away and then arrange another meeting to inform them that it is inappropriate to walk out of a meeting about work. You should explain that such a meeting is a reasonable management request and walking out before it has concluded could result in disciplinary action. Let them know that disciplinary action is not the intention at this stage, as it's happened once, but warn them that disciplinary action is possible should it happen again. I would follow up this reprimand in writing, making the point that the letter is not part of any formal process. I include the following sentence at the end of such an email in case the situation repeats or escalates and your account is challenged at a later date:

'Please let me know by the end of this week if you feel that this is not an accurate record of our meeting.'

You could do all of the above in writing, but my preference is a face-to-face meeting, if possible, with a written message to follow up.

You need to establish that their behaviour is not an acceptable response and that there are consequences. These consequences are not going to be applied this first time but, if it happens again, they know what actions might follow.

What if they don't say anything?

These conversations, no matter how friendly, can trigger a defensive reaction. Like all mammals, we instinctively react to a threat with either a fight-or-flight response or, in some cases, we 'freeze': some prey animals hold still and hide in the camouflage so the predator doesn't see them.

In the same way, some humans shut down and can't move or speak up when they feel threatened. This response can be quite confusing. What do you do when the person refuses to speak?

Hold the silence

If you have sight of a clock you will notice that time will warp and ten seconds will feel like an agonising ten minutes. Hold the silence because they might be thinking or they might be being stroppy but, either way, you want to let them break the silence. If you get to two minutes (which is highly unlikely) you might say something like: 'Would you share with me your thoughts on how we can achieve ... the outcome?' Encourage them to snap out of the 'freeze' and express themselves, but avoid filling the silence yourself.

Emotions are a core component of difficult conversations with the interplay of ego states of Parent and Child – defensive reactions as well as genuine emotional release from pent-up stress. I hope you can see there are ways to manage these reactions more effectively by developing your skills. Don't give yourself a hard time if you're not executing all of this 'perfectly'. As I've said earlier, there's no such thing as a perfect difficult conversation. We can only do our best, with this insight into human behaviour, to manage each conversation.

Chapter 7: Ensuring the conversation creates positive change

In this chapter, we find out:
· How you are sabotaging yourself.
· How to reduce your workload in a difficult conversation.
· How to make positive change more likely to happen.

Groundhog Day

Have you ever had a difficult conversation where the person seems to agree with everything you say and when they walk out of the room you think to yourself: 'They're not going to do any of it'? This is a common problem. And it doesn't end there.

Difficult conversations can be like the film *Groundhog Day* (Ramis, 1993), starring Bill Murray and Andie MacDowell. Phil (Bill Murray) is stuck reliving the same day (when the groundhog emerges from hibernation), until he overcomes his character flaws and wins the girl. This very funny film has given us the phrase 'Groundhog Day', meaning endlessly repeating the same event.

If action isn't taken after a difficult conversation you could find yourself having another conversation … and another one, and yet another. It can feel like your very own repetitious version of *Groundhog Day* where you're trying different approaches but waking up to face the same conversation again.

One reason why resolving difficult conversations quickly is part of our success criteria is because we only have so much energy for these demanding conversations and, as we repeat the same conversation with the same person, we lose patience and become exasperated.

> *Conversation 1: You're fully behind supporting them to resolve the issue.*
>
> *Conversation 2: You're still behind them but can't understand why more progress on the issue hasn't been made.*
>
> *Conversation 3: You want them to improve but you're getting frustrated.*
>
> *Conversation 4: You're getting bored and fed up with this because the change isn't happening.*
>
> *Conversation 5: You've had enough! Why haven't they fixed this?*

Have you experienced or witnessed any 'Groundhog Day' conversations?

In Chapter 2 we looked at your return on invested time. In the scenario above these conversations would amount to a least an hour, probably more, with zero return because, after five conversations, there has been no improvement. (You might even say you've got a negative return!)

To reduce this issue, you need to build trust in the interaction.

You are inadvertently sabotaging your message

It's not what you say, it's how you say it.

Albert Mehrabian (1981) researched how people communicate when they are sharing feelings or attitudes and this is what he found:

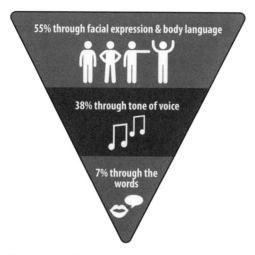

Figure 17: The split of non-verbal and verbal communication when communicating attitudes and feelings (Mehrabian, 1981)

What do you focus on before going into a difficult conversation? Most people think about the words they will use, not their non-verbal communication. Of course your choice of words is important, but if your body language doesn't support your message then you might not be heard. Think of body language and tone of voice, which make up 93% of this communication, as being like white noise. The worse they are, the louder the white noise and, thus, the harder it is to hear what you are actually saying. The better they are, the quieter the white noise and, in this case, the easier it is hear your message. We want to ensure your 7% of words are 100% heard. We can only do that by managing your non-verbal communication.

We are usually stressed and anxious in a difficult conversation and this stress can leak out in our body language. The problem is we can't control how our non-verbal signals are perceived or interpreted by the other person.

Our brains are wired to read non-verbal communication

It is fascinating how astute we are at picking up moods, like walking into a room of people and feeling an 'atmosphere'. We may detect that the tension in the room could be cut with a knife, or pick up an air of playful mischief in the group, or a positive vibe of friendly connection, often without a word being said. The molecules in the room haven't changed, they are just the same, but you can feel the atmosphere, sometimes more clearly than if someone tried to articulate the group dynamics.

This is our limbic brain at work and it is brilliant at reading and interpreting these subtle clues. No matter what you do, the limbic brain will be looking, analysing and interpreting non-verbal behaviour, sometimes correctly, sometimes not. You can't change this constant human brain activity and so you need to make sure your verbal and non-verbal communication match.

Building trust in the interaction

Managing your non-verbal body language is all about building rapport with the other person to create a safe place for the conversation. You build rapport, without thinking, when you're comfortable with someone; however, when you're stressed or anxious, your discomfort shows in your non-verbal body language and this means there's no rapport between you. 'Rapport' is a French word that means connection, bonding, empathy, affinity and a sense of camaraderie.

Rapport makes the interaction more trusting and honest, and it makes the other person more comfortable than they would have been. As leading coach Tony Robbins says:

> 'Rapport is the ability to enter someone else's world, to make him feel that you understand him, that you have a strong common bond.' (2012, p.68)

The beauty of rapport is that it can make *you* feel more comfortable as well and help you manage your emotions. And, once you have built rapport with someone else, you will have a more relaxed connection without thinking about it, just like when you are with friends.

The four Ss of rapport

You can build rapport by working through the four Ss:

Stance

This is the simplest yet most powerful way to establish rapport; simply adopt the same posture, sitting or standing, just like the other person.

If they have their legs crossed, you cross your legs. If their hands are on their lap, place your hands on your lap. If they change how they are sitting, you should too. You are *mirroring* the person.

Don't worry about which leg is crossed over which, you're simply trying to echo their shape. However, don't sit in a way that is uncomfortable or unnatural to you because this will look contrived and undermine rapport.

You might feel doing this mirroring is really obvious, but it's not to the other person (unless you do it really badly!) Remember, you already do this when you're talking to someone in a comfortable interaction, without realising it.

Signal

'Signal' means mirroring specific gestures. If the other person is resting their head on their hand, you might too. Don't worry about which hand they are using. If they circle their hands when talking about things 'going round and round', then you might do this same gesture at some point in the conversation. As with mirroring posture, don't use any gesture that doesn't feel natural to you.

Say

This is a simple and powerful way of building rapport: use *their* words. Nothing tells someone that you've heard them like saying what they have said. So, if they say they are 'frustrated' you can refer to them being 'frustrated', not 'confused' or 'finding it hard'. If they use a specific turn of phrase you can repeat it back, for example: 'So you feel like you're *out of your depth* with this report writing'. Show them you are listening to what they are saying. This is one of the skills of active listening.

Summarise

It can be very powerful to summarise the other person's main points. It shows you've been listening closely and allows you to check your understanding and correct your comprehension of their viewpoint, if necessary.

All four Ss build bridges with the other person. You don't have to put all of them in place in every conversation, but try to use 'Stance' and at least one other skill and you will find that your difficult conversations will improve.

You're not a parrot looking in the mirror

It's crucial you remain true to your own natural style when building rapport because our limbic systems kick off when we sense someone is not being genuine. This isn't about you being a parrot, repeating back everything that is said, while acting like a human mirror to the other person. It's about sending out a subconscious signal to say: 'Look, we're just the same, you and I'.

Common questions about body language

In the many years I've been training people on how to have successful difficult conversations, I've been asked a lot of questions about body language. Here are the most common ones.

What if their body language is negative?

This is the question I'm asked the most. Not everyone sits nicely during a difficult conversation! This is understandable, and often you can be challenged to mirror negative body language. In this case, don't sit exactly like the other person, sit like a positive version of them. For example, if someone is defensively sitting with their arms folded, you can have your arms folded in a similar, but more relaxed, manner.

Activity 14: Go online to see how to manage negative body language

Go to www.ukheadsup.com/negativebodylanguage/ where I'll show you how to positively mirror negative body language (a far better medium than explaining in writing).

Sitting in a 'neutral' way

Some people sit in a very particular way to neutralise their body language. The problem is that when this is different to the other person they don't neutralise the negative posture, they just fail to build rapport and the two people remain disconnected and oppositional.

It's impossible *not* to communicate.

Whichever way you sit or stand you are sending out messages. To reduce the white noise this can create and let your words get through, you need to build rapport through mirroring body language.

What if they fidget?
Try to assume their overall shape but do not try to mirror their fidgeting. They will probably settle after a while and you can readjust your position then. The danger is that if you try to mirror them as they fidget, you'll feel like you're both doing some kind of bad boy band dance routine! Your actions will look comical and the other person is likely to feel that you are mocking them.

Classic body language mistakes to avoid
When it comes to body language there are mistakes I've seen enough times to consider them worth mentioning. These points might seem minor, but people are always amazed at the impact they have on the success of a difficult conversation.

Watch your back
The position of your back makes a difference when building rapport as it changes the overall shape of the interaction and reduces the symmetry and the mirroring. If the other person is leaning back and you're leaning forward, then you're not mirroring. It sounds insignificant but it can have a big impact on the feel of the conversation.

The wounded animal
I see this most with legs but it can happen with arms as well. With legs, one leg is back, looking almost as if it's wounded. With arms, the pose is one arm across the body and lap and the other protectively in front. Avoid these postures as they send a message of vulnerability.

Footloose and fancy free
Watch your feet. When they are tucked back and under your chair, crossed or uncrossed, they are conveying that you are not comfortable with the situation and this weakens your message. You want to match the other person but, if this is hard, sit with your feet firmly on the floor, with your knees and feet at right angles.

Positive body language leads to greater success and allows your words to be heard; it builds trust in the interaction, which provides the foundation for making positive change happen.

There is another important skill for making positive change happen: the power of questioning and listening, which builds more rapport and advances the issue towards resolution.

Questioning and listening to create positive change

As a qualified coach, I'm a big fan of questioning and listening techniques because they are so powerful in creating long-lasting change. Good questions and listening skills let the other person do the work, which is where the work should be done. After all, this process is about their improvement and we are there to help them along the way, but not do the work for them. I love witnessing this personal empowerment through successful difficult conversations.

School leaders tell me they feel like they are forever solving problems across the entire school and that much of this onerous responsibility is unnecessary, especially when staff members come to them with an issue because they are sidestepping the responsibility of decision-making. That might be the right call in some cases, but it happens more often than it should.

If you experience this syndrome, as a leader, then these questioning and listening techniques will alleviate the burden of constantly being the problem solver and will support your team in finding their own effective answers.

Four levels of questioning and listening

Figure 18 shows the four levels of questioning. It's unlikely you'll need all these levels for the easier difficult conversations (like lateness) but they can prove fundamental to achieving success with the mid- and high-level conversations.

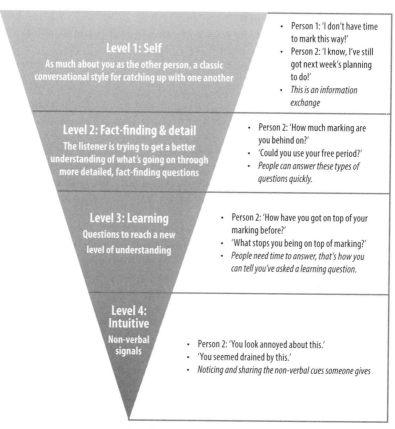

Figure 18: Four levels of questioning and listening

Using Level 1 and 2 questions

Level 1 questions are an information exchange (such as a 'How was your day?' conversation).

Level 2 questions are about finding out facts (like getting holiday tips from a friend).

Both have their place and can be a good foundation for the rest of the conversation. However, this can be a safe haven in a difficult conversation and I've seen lots of people retreat to this place. Be careful not to stay in these question zones, especially if you're dealing with a mid- or high-level difficult conversation about performance or conduct.

The power of Level 3 questions

Level 3 questions are learning questions, specifically prompting learning for the other person. They tend to be open questions and the hallmark of asking one is that the other person needs to stop and think about it. When you land one of these wonderful questions, wait quietly while the other person is thinking. If you speak, you will interrupt their thoughts. You know when someone is thinking because their eyes will be moving around.

How do you know what questions to ask? Well, this is where the listening aspect comes in because, often, the question you ask is based on what they have told you and the outcome you're working towards.

Level 3 questions help you achieve the outcome because they are questions that get the person to think about what is causing the issue, what they are finding hard, why it's such a challenge and how they might overcome it.

Level 4 questions can break an impasse

Level 4 questions can be powerful in breaking an impasse or moving a conversation forward. They are about observing and sharing non-verbal communication and allow us to bring important, unspoken parts of the conversation to the fore.

- We might feel someone is upset because their eyes have become glassy.
- We might notice someone is looking angry.
- We might be feeling angry or upset ourselves.

Whatever the emotion, sharing the fact that we are noticing it, without judgement, can really help in getting someone to explain what is creating the emotion and helps to move the issue forward. For example:

- I get the impression you are angry about this.
- I'm noticing you seem to be upset.
- Would I be right in saying this is frustrating you?

It's important to deliver these words in an adult way and to state the emotion without a judgemental tone.

Questioning and listening are skills that need to be practised; their mastery requires consistent work over time, until this style of communicating becomes natural and intuitive.

Practice makes perfect

The great thing about rapport is that you don't have to wait for a difficult conversation to practise the skills. You can practise them in non-difficult, 'low-cost' situations, which can feel a lot safer.

A low-cost situation is one where you need to have a low-level difficult conversation with someone you are likely to never see again; for example, when out for a meal and you believe your wine is corked or your meal is cold. This is a great time to practise some of these rapport skills, like the four Ss, especially 'Say' and 'Summarise'.

A mid-cost situation is when you have a tougher message to give to someone you're unlikely to see again (for example, a serious customer complaint). This is a great place to practise the four Ss and the questioning and listening techniques discussed earlier.

A high-cost situation is a difficult conversation with people you will see again (such as your team).

As you can see the 'cost' is elevated in these situations; firstly, by seeing the person again and, secondly, by how difficult the message is to deliver.

Activity 15: Practise building rapport in a safe space

To help you be more aware of low-cost practise opportunities going forward, take a moment to think of two low-cost opportunities you've recently had where you would have been able to practise your rapport skills.

Chapter 8: Structuring the conversation for success

In this chapter, we look at:
- How to structure a difficult conversation.
- How to follow up in writing.
- What to do when a conversation comes at you and you haven't had time to prepare.

STORM structure

My structure for navigating difficult conversations is based on the acronym STORM. The steps remind us why these conversations are so important, by referring back to Tuckman's theory of group development. Here is how it works.

State the issue

This is where you say your opening sentence (I, issue, the outcome), prepared beforehand and with examples, if necessary, as covered in detail in Chapter 5.

You need to deliver this in an adult voice with your non-verbal communication mirroring theirs.

Their side

It's important to gauge how the other person views the situation, so hand over the conversation to them, with something like:

'What are your thoughts?'

'How do you see this?'

People are likely to react, which can be uncomfortable so remember:

People are entitled to their reaction.

And some level of reaction is inevitable, so accept it will happen. Keeping this in mind will help you during this part of the conversation.

If you realise you're not mirroring them, now is a good time to readjust your body language and use the other skills of building rapport: use their words, summarise and make great use of your questioning and listening skills (particularly Level 3 and 4 – see Figure 18). Remember to keep a check on any 'parent' or 'child' feelings stirring within you.

Options

Here you move into a collaborative problem-solving stage: How *could* we improve this issue? You can simply bat around ideas without committing to any solutions.

Questioning and listening can be very powerful in this stage.

Resolution

Now, you want them to decide:

1. What is going to be done to improve the situation?

2. Who is going to do it?

3. When will they do it by?

Have you ever come out of a conversation with a long list of things to do? This happens a lot and it's the wrong way around. We compensate for the conversation being difficult by taking on more than we need to. You should come away with actions that *only* you can do. The actions are meant to be about *their* improvement, so they must take ownership. Taking action will show you their degree of commitment to improving. So, typically, their list should be longer than yours.

Move on and follow up

This stage is easy to miss out but do not overlook it.

Move on

Acknowledge that the conversation was hard but also note some of the positives. Maybe mention that the actions are good ideas, or that you both have a better understanding of the issue now, through your honest dialogue.

This is an important step in creating an ongoing culture of healthy conflict.

Follow up

Even if you're able to resolve the crux of the issue in one conversation (which is always the aim) you will still need a follow up, so arrange a time to meet again to see how the actions are progressing. This leaves the door open on the conversation, gives you permission to go back to it and shows that you will be checking in and making them accountable. How soon the meeting is scheduled depends on what's appropriate for the issue.

The next meeting

When you follow up on the conversation, if the issue hasn't improved then, with your clear outcome, look at what could be done now, using the STORM structure again.

If they have done everything and improved the issue then this is an opportunity to congratulate them, make the point that although it was a tough conversation, it has led to something better for them personally and for the school. Flag up that if you see the problem reoccurring you'll raise it with them, to stop it escalating again. This statement lets them know they need to maintain the standard.

Activity 16: Go online to learn more about the STORM structure

You can access a free, short video e-course taking you through the STORM structure at www.ukheadsup.com/storm/

State Issue
- Tell them the issue early in the conversation using 'I, issue, the outcome'.
- Have examples of the issue.

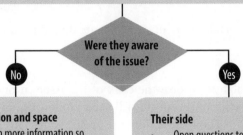

Were they aware of the issue?

No

Yes

Give information and space
- Offer them more information so they can understand.

Their side
- Open questions to let them give their viewpoint.

Postpone
- Arrange another time to meet.

Yes

Do they need some time to reflect

No

Options – Work together for a solution
- 'How can we resolve/improve this?'
- Do not fix the problem for them, they have to own it, but you can support them.

Resolution – agree next steps
- Agree on what actions will be taken:
    - What they will do and by when.
    - Any actions for you.

Move on – Close and follow up
- Acknowledge positives: 'I'm really glad we could discuss this issue. It was great how you (positive aspect of their contribution/behaviour)'.
- Agree how you will monitor/follow up their progress

Figure 19: STORM structure for difficult conversations

For low-level conversations, such as lateness, you might find you only need 'S', 'T' and 'M'; it's unlikely you'll need to go into 'Options'. For mid- and high-level conversations, you will need the full structure.

Don't rush to the end
The STORM structure is a sequential structure and you need to secure each stage before moving on.

'Stating the issue' and 'Their side' allow the person to understand and accept the issue of concern. There is no point moving on to 'Options' if this agreement isn't in place. However, there can be a temptation to move on to 'Options' and 'Resolution' because we feel like we're taking action and action feels good. Resist this temptation. If all that comes from your first meeting is that the other person understands and accepts the issue, then you have done well. You can then meet again and work on the 'Options' and 'Resolution' from the strong platform you've created.

A well-structured and well-delivered message can yield surprising results. Here's the email I received from one senior leader after our training.

'Just wanted to let you know that I've just had my difficult conversation. It went incredibly well! The member of staff THANKED me for bringing it to their attention and admitted that he'd been coasting!'

Written follow up
It's good to follow up a difficult conversation in writing to:

1. Provide you both with a summary of what was said, which you can refer to if needed.

2. Have a paper trail in case you need to move into capability in the future.

The most important of these reasons is the first one; however, if things don't improve you will be glad there is documentation of the support you put in place.

I know you're busy and so here's an easy and quick template to use when sending the follow up.

Dear [Name],

Thank you for meeting with me [today/date]. [As mentioned/I thought] a summary would be useful for both of us.

We met because [I, issue, the outcome].

We agreed [resolutions: who, what, when by].

We will meet again on [follow-up date].

I hope you agree this is an accurate reflection of our meeting; if you do not please let me know by [date – typically a week].

[Your sign off]

Figure 20: Template for written follow up after a difficult conversation
(not for formal meetings)

You can access this follow up as a template at www.ukheadsup.com/sdcfollowupemail

You can add more if you want to, but this template provides the most basic summary of what was said in the dialogue. The last sentence is carefully worded so as not to ask for agreement by a set date, but to ask for any *disagreement* by that date. This means that inaction by them is an action; if you don't hear back you could assume that they agree. Please be aware that this is **not** a template for any formal capability or disciplinary letters.

What if a conversation lands on you?

So far, I've shown you how to prepare for a difficult conversation that you have decided you need to have. But confrontations are not all planned and you can be 'ambushed' at any time!

The classic 'Have you got a minute?' request can often be the opening to a difficult conversation you haven't planned for! So, what do you do? There is only **one** difference in how you approach this spontaneous difficult conversation and everything else remains the same process. The slight difference occurs in your opening sentence; your *'I, issue, the outcome'*. You can't prepare this when someone approaches you out of the blue, but what you can do is work out their sentence. This creates clarity because people don't usually come to us with a clear idea of their goal. They usually focus on the issue, not the outcome. If they do have an outcome it's often not the real outcome, it's a solution. For example, if a parent wants a boy moved from her son's class because he's bullying him, this looks like an outcome but really it is a 'solution siren'. The real desired outcome is for her son to be happy at school, which might be achieved in alternative, better ways.

In spending a little time working out their 'I, issue, the outcome', you can ensure that they feel listened to and the chat will allow you to gather a lot of information (their side) without necessarily having to solve the problem at this stage (of course, if it's easily fixed then do so). Once you've figured out the problem say it back to them to check you've got it right. At that point you have a choice: have the conversation now, or have the conversation another time, using the STORM structure and the opening sentence *you've* worked out for them.

Whenever you decide to have the conversation you can use the STORM process just as I have outlined. The only difference from everything I've covered so far is that you have clarified their *'I, issue, the outcome'* sentence and you begin with this; the rest follows the same process.

Structuring your conversation well, especially the opening few sentences, will increase the success of your conversation and reduce your stress because you will know the path you're navigating. Remember that your non-verbal communication and emotional management throughout this encounter is crucial if you want your message to be heard. You can structure your conversation perfectly but, if you don't have all three components in place, it will not be as effective.

Chapter 9: Adapting your approach for success

In this chapter, we learn about:
· Different approaches to increase the success of your difficult conversations.
· How to know which approach will work best.

Knowing the best approach for each individual can be tricky. Should you tell them what to do or coach them? We all have our favourite approaches. You might have learnt several communication styles but most of us tend to have one strong preference. The more stressful a situation, the more likely that style is to show up. That's great if you default to the best approach for that conversation, but not so good if you slip into an unhelpful communication style under stress.

How do you enter the conversation knowing the best approach to use?

Four leadership styles

There are many theories of leadership and many terms for different leadership approaches. The skill/will matrix (Landsberg, 2003) and its leadership styles are easy to use and support difficult conversations.

The skills of building rapport, questioning and listening are coaching skills that work well as a broad-brush tool in most situations. The skill/will model allows us to fine tune our approach in order to resolve the issue more quickly and effectively.

This method is based on the competency curve:

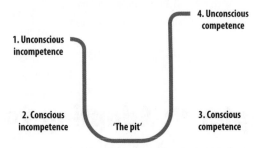

Figure 21: The competency curve

You might be familiar with the competency curve already but, if not, I will explain the concept. When I've explained this in schools, eyes light up as people recognise where they are (or have been) on the curve and realise that each stage was part of a learning journey.

1. Unconscious incompetence

This is where we don't know what we don't know, a place where 'ignorance is bliss'.

A good example of this curve at work is learning to drive a car. When I was learning to drive, my dad insisted that I have my first lesson with him on my seventeenth birthday. He'd got everything lined up – L-plates on, provisional driving licence ready – and he was excited. I was excited too. But I wasn't in a rush to get in the car because I thought I'd be driving in no time (and I wanted to eat more birthday cake!)

I remember thinking: 'Anyone can drive a car, it's not hard. Put your foot down and turn the wheel.' That was until I sat in the driver's seat for the first time!

2. Conscious incompetence

This is where we know what we don't know. We can now see the void in our knowledge and/or skills and realise that to plug that gap will take time and effort.

The first time I sat in the driver's seat of my dad's red Renault 5, I looked down and saw three pedals. *Three*? What was third one for? What does a clutch do? After I bunny hopped the car around an empty car park, trying to find the mythical 'biting point', I found myself thinking 'I'm going to be the *only* person who *can't* drive!' I'd left unconscious incompetence and landed firmly in conscious incompetence.

John Hattie calls this place 'the pit'; it's the place where our learning becomes challenging. We don't have to learn and we could abandon this competency curve, but we might choose to push on to learn new skills. The pit sounds like quite a depressing place so bear in mind that while it can be hard it's not always a plummet into the abyss – it can be more like a skirmish.

3. **Conscious competence**

This is where we know what we know. At this stage of learning, we can perform the skill but we have to actively think about each step.

Thankfully I had a patient father who spent many hours teaching me how to drive until I could do it. I had to concentrate, though, and if he tried to start a conversation I'd tell him not to talk to me because I couldn't drive and talk. The act of driving needed all my attention and so it took up a lot of my cognitive function.

4. **Unconscious competence**

At this final stage of learning, you don't know what you know. Competence is automatic and flows naturally and we take our knowledge and skills for granted. Here, we can perform tasks without active thought.

Like all experienced drivers, when I drive my car I'm not thinking about driving, at least not consciously. I can think about my day and what I'm planning for the weekend, and I can pay more attention to what's going on around me on the road, rather than the act of driving itself. I can perform this task automatically, without conscious thought.

You will have experienced the competency curve in many ways, perhaps when you started teaching or leading a core subject, or when you've learnt a new skill or taken up a new hobby.

Competency curves are higher on one side, because when you get to unconscious competence you have a higher level of skill than when you started and so curves build on one another as our skills continue to grow, as shown in Figure 22.

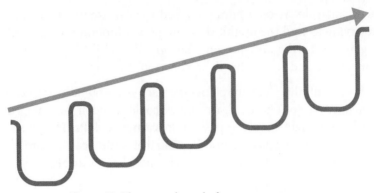

Figure 22: The upward trend of competency curves

The skill/will matrix

The skill/will matrix takes the competency curve and helps us understand what the other person needs from us. It looks at two variables, someone's skill and someone's will, so that we can identify which approach is likely to work best for them and resolve the issue more quickly and effectively.

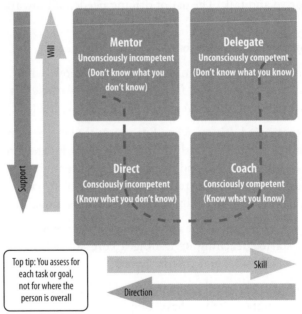

Figure 23: The skill/will matrix (Landsberg, 2003)

Four approaches to support the four stages of the competency curve

At each stage of the curve a different approach works best.

1. **Mentor someone who is unconsciously incompetent (high will, low skill)**

Someone who needs mentoring will have high will and low skill. They will be motivated but lacking some of the skills they need to be fully competent.

NQTs are a good example of this stage: they are usually motivated and can't wait to have their own class and classroom but they have not had enough experience to really hone their craft. While they have theory and basic skills, they lack sufficient skills to teach at a competent level.

A mentor is someone who can perform the role they are mentoring extremely well. They bring with them experience and knowledge to guide the mentee when needed. When we mentor we use a blend of coaching questions, such as:

How is it going?

What areas do you want to focus on to improve your teaching?

And some directing questions when we need to give the mentee a nudge in the right direction:

I've noticed that your maths planning isn't as detailed as it needs to be for maximum learning. How are you finding maths?

Coaching questions tap into their motivation and own analysis, while directing points them towards areas they need to develop in, but might not realise.

2. **Directing someone who is consciously incompetent (low will, low skill)**

Someone who needs directing will have low will and low skill. They have become aware of their skill/knowledge gap and will be in 'the pit'.

It might be that your recently qualified teacher (RQT) realises their behaviour strategies don't work consistently and that they need to learn new ones. It may be that a new literacy leader discovers that getting the teaching team on board with their initiative isn't as easy as just asking them.

Directing is the best option here: the person hasn't developed the skill sufficiently and they need training and support from someone who has.

Telling someone what to do (directing) has a bad reputation because if used at the wrong time it can feel patronising. However, when someone is struggling in a place of conscious incompetence, directing is the best approach.

3. **Coaching someone who is consciously competent (low will, high skill)**

When someone has low will and high skill, coaching is the best approach because they will be skilled but lacking motivation.

They might be a great teacher who has 'gone off the boil'. You know they can do the job because you've seen them in action, but they just don't seem to be performing well now.

In this case, coaching works because someone in this quadrant doesn't need to learn new skills; they have them already, but they need to understand why they are not motivated and what they can do about it. That's not something you can tell them, it's something you can help them figure out through coaching questions.

A mistake that leaders make when someone is in this place of low motivation is telling them how to do the skill they are no longer demonstrating. It's an easy mistake to make because the skill is the more tangible aspect and training someone in a skill is easier than helping them understand why they are not motivated. However, this can really backfire because the person has the skill and being told what to do can turn them off.

Coaching is not only for unmotivated people. It's a great tool for three of these four quadrants, the exception being when someone needs directing. When I coach people, they are often in the delegate quadrant: highly motivated and highly skilled.

4. Delegating to someone who is unconsciously competent (high will, high skill)

Someone you can reliably delegate work to possesses high will and high skill.

They will have demonstrated the skills and/or knowledge required to do the task you want them to take on.

Maybe they were a talented literacy leader and now you want them to lead another area. It might be that they are a whizz at using class data to improve progress and you want them to do the same across another phase or year group.

When we truly delegate we let the other person take control and ownership of the area because, hopefully, they are better at the role than we are. They can set the goals, work out the timeline of when to touch base with you and decide what success looks like. That doesn't mean that you can't apply parameters or share your thoughts; however, your involvement should be a discussion with the other person taking the lead. This is true delegation.

Another angle to delegation is when we delegate tasks to others because it makes more sense for their time to be used than yours. An example might be a headteacher delegating diary management to a member of the admin team so that they have more time for essential tasks.

I know you've been told to delegate more, but don't! You can only delegate to people who are competent at that skill. When you delegate to someone who is not, you'll often find yourself thinking: 'It would be have been easier to do it myself'.

Using the skill/will matrix for maximum effect
Here are some tips for getting the best results from this model.

1. Focus on a specific task – be micro not macro

While someone might sit in a quadrant overall, when you're assessing someone's competence try to focus on the specific task that needs doing. If a teacher isn't teaching well, ask yourself what it is exactly that is holding them back: pace, planning, marking? Then think about where they sit on the matrix for that specific task. They might be brilliant at behaviour management (delegate) but weak and unmotivated at marking (directing).

I can drive a car and you can delegate to me to get you to a destination, but put me in the cockpit of an airborne plane and I will be screaming for direction!

2.   **Tell people if you're going to use a different approach**

If you've decided you need to use a different approach, talk to the other person and share with them what you're thinking and why.

Activity 17: What approach do they need from me?

Think of a difficult conversation you need to have. You might like to use ones you thought about for **Activity 5: Who and what difficult conversations do you have?** on page 43.

Apply the skill/will matrix to see what approach you think will work best in that difficult conversation.

Who	Issue with their performance or conduct? (P or C)	What is it specifically about?	Importance rating (1 not very, 4 critical)	Skill: High or low	Will: High or low	Approach

---

When I first learnt this model, I was working at the John Lewis head office with a team of three senior leaders reporting to me. I looked at the model and realised I was using my preferred approach, coaching, with all of them. However, each of them needed one of the other approaches. When I went back to the office I shared what I'd learned and, individually, asked them if they would prefer me to use a different, more appropriate approach. It was a resounding yes!

Improving your difficult conversations

Before you go into a difficult conversation think about which approach is most likely to work best for the person and this *specific* situation. We're all in different quadrants for different things and the skill is working out which approach is most appropriate for the conversation you need to have. The coaching skills of rapport, questioning and listening will make most difficult conversations more effective for you. Indeed, you will need to use these skills no matter what approach the skill/will matrix says is best. The skill/will matrix lets you fine tune your approach with a slightly different shade, to increase the success of your difficult conversations, making them better suited to each person.

In the STORM structure, you can bring in the most appropriate approach you have chosen at the 'Options' stage.

Options – depending on the approach you have chosen you might choose to tell them some options (directing); you might help them find their own options (coaching); you might do a bit of both (mentoring); or you might let them lead and decide what they think is the best way forward (delegate).

You may have spotted the bonus of this matrix: it works well for any development conversation, not just the difficult ones. As one deputy head said to me: 'I adapt my approach to children all the time, but I've never thought about adapting my approach for adults.'

Chapter 10:
Ten common problems and how to avoid them

In this chapter, we uncover:
· How to have a difficult conversation with a work colleague who is also a friend.
· What to do if you can't agree.
· How to deal with distractions.
· How to get someone to take the issue seriously and take action to improve it.
· The nearest thing to a panacea in difficult conversations.

There's an abundance of tools that can help you with a variety of problems in difficult conversations. In this chapter, I share ten of the most effective tools for problems I come across all the time.

Activity 18: What are your most common problems?

It helps to know which problems you experience most during difficult conversations. Look at the list below and self-assess which of them you experience most, by highlighting the three most common for you.

1. They don't hear what I want them to hear.

2. They always change the subject.

3. They agree with me, but don't take any action to change.

4. We don't agree and can't move forward.

5. They ask, 'Who told you that?', but I can't tell them.

6. Having a difficult conversation with a colleague who is also a friend.

7. At staff meetings the only people who don't respond to issues are the people who need to!

8. The conversation gets heated or emotional.

9. They say nothing and keep silent.

1. Opening the conversation

I can't talk about the most common problems without reiterating that the single biggest mistake is failing to start the conversation well. That is:

1. Having the conversation that really needs to be had, without getting drawn off track.

2. Starting with a clearly structured sentence that you have prepared.

None of these ten tools will work if you don't have a clear opening sentence with a specific outcome.

2. Quick-fire distractions

Have you ever had one of those difficult conversations where you raise your issue and the other person then raises a list of their own issues, such as the way children are behaving, the fact no one tidies the staff room, that TAs are taking longer breaks, or that staff meetings are too long?

Typically, you start to discuss these issues, explore their concerns, and make notes so you can deal with them. At the end of the conversation you realise you got sidetracked and didn't get to talk about the issue you had raised in the first place!

The reaction from the other person is like an animal that has been cornered, lashing out for an escape. This defensive tactic is understandable but unhelpful. If these issues were so important why didn't they raise them before? Most likely, these issues have been thrown up as a defence mechanism, a distraction to draw you off on a tangent. If you follow this sidetrack you will delay dealing with the bigger issue.

Here is how you can manage this.

1. Listen to what they are saying, make a note of each issue if you want to, but don't start discussing them.

2. Then say: 'I'm happy to talk about all of these issues with you in another meeting. Today, I've called this meeting to talk about your *"I, issue, the outcome* sentence".'

In my experience, they never arrange that meeting.

3. They are not taking action
In Chapter 3, I talked about the idea of 'two-worlds' to help you decide if you really need to have the conversation. This idea of 'two-worlds' is also useful when someone either doesn't realise how important the issue is or you find they are not taking action after a few conversations.

We help them see the two-worlds we are heading towards (see Figure 6):

One is currently being walked towards, where the problem isn't resolved. What does that future look like?

The other is where the issue is resolved and there is a happier future.

I was working with a leadership team in a 'Requires Improvement' (RI) school. The entire school team was working hard to improve and the leaders were having many difficult conversations. One leader had been working with a teacher for quite some time trying to improve the quality of their teaching to 'Good'. She'd put a lot of energy into this, really wanting to help the teacher improve, but it wasn't working. There were occasional glimmers of hope, but they would quickly fade. To this leader's credit she'd had far more than five conversations and was still committed to helping this teacher but was worn down, not knowing what else to do.

I talked the leader through the two-worlds technique and, in this instance, the negative future was going into formal capability while the positive was having the teacher perform at a consistently 'Good' level. She would need to say this explicitly to the teacher so that she could understand the seriousness of the situation and that the extra support and all the difficult conversations were aimed at avoiding her going into capability. Without her teaching improving she would, sadly, find herself in capability. The leader did go pale at the thought of having this conversation. It's not a nice one to have, so I modelled it for her.

At our next training session, I caught up with the school leaders on how their difficult conversations were going and this one leader in particular had seen a dramatic turn around after a 'two-worlds' conversation. The teacher in question was improving and, within a few months, she was a consistently 'Good' teacher and had maintained that standard.

This is not an unusual situation. I see this problem a lot and explaining the two-worlds technique can help someone see the importance of the need to change. As hard as it might be to have a 'two-worlds' conversation it's far worse to let someone walk out of a conversation not fully appreciating the seriousness of the situation and, therefore, not putting in the necessary effort. Ultimately, they might not want to change, but that is their choice. We have to help them see the choice and the consequences. Sadly, people are often surprised to find themselves in capability because they've not realised they've been heading towards that future for some time. Then, 'suddenly', they find themselves facing this ordeal and that's not fair on them.

4. What if they don't hear what I'm telling them?

Even with a perfectly constructed opening sentence there is a (smaller) risk that the person doesn't hear what you're telling them. If this happens try the 'broken record' technique; it works by simply repeating your outcome.

> *Person 1: I can't mark my books every day!*
>
> *Person 2: I do need you to follow the marking policy and this means marking every day.*
>
> *Person 1: There's not enough time to do it.*
>
> *Person 2: I understand you feel there's not enough time; however, I do need you to follow the marking policy and this means marking every day.*
>
> *Person 1: I don't know how I'm going to fit it in.*
>
> *Person 2: Perhaps we can talk about how you can fit it in, because I do need you to follow the marking policy and this means marking every day.*

This technique is about being clear that the outcome must be achieved and then helping the person find a way to achieve it. This 'broken record' technique is a useful tool for your non-negotiable policies.

5. What if we can't agree?

Another common problem is when agreement can't be reached. Maybe a parent is adamantly against their child having an assessment for dyslexia or autism or a teacher refuses to follow the marking policy. You can find yourself with your metaphorical horns locked and the conversation can't progress.

When this happens, it can be useful to 'chunk up': that is, you move the conversation to a higher conceptual level. Let me demonstrate this with two examples – the higher conceptual level is underlined.

Example 1:

Parent: She doesn't need an assessment, there's nothing wrong with her.

You: Mrs Jones, I think we both want your daughter to do well in school, to be happy and to learn as well as she can. Would you agree?

Parent: Well yes, of course I do!

You: Great, me too. I'm worried that if we don't have the assessment we might not know all the ways we can help her do her best and that would mean she wouldn't learn as well as she can because we wouldn't know how best to support her.

Example 2:

Teacher: I can't mark my books every day!

You: Jane, I think you're a conscientious teacher who wants to do well for your children. Am I right in thinking this?

Teacher: I'd like to think I am.

You: I think you are too. However, I can't understand how not marking their books fits with this? I appreciate time is short and I'd like to help you find a way to make time to mark their books and be the conscientious teacher I know you to be.

We move from the lower issue (assessment, marking), up to a higher level (daughter to do well, conscientious teacher), then back to the lower issue. This often clears the way to move the issue forward because it creates agreement.

6. Who told you? How do you know?

As a leader, you are not going to witness everything that happens in your school. This means that your difficult conversations can be about things you have been told but not seen. This is fine, as it's part of your leadership responsibility and there is an expectation that staff can come and report things they are not happy about. What can happen when you have this conversation is the other person asks: 'Who told you?' There are several ways to respond to this.

- If the person who told you is happy for you to say it was them, and you feel it's appropriate, then you can.

- If you were told in confidence then you can say: 'I was told in confidence and so I can't disclose this.'
- If they persist in wanting to know, you can say: 'The issue is not who told me, the issue is…' (and then whatever your 'I, issue, the outcome' sentence is).

7. Difficult conversations with a colleague who is also a friend

We often become friends with people we work with; it's nice, but can mean that if we need to have a difficult conversation with them it's harder. It might be a difficult conversation with a friend who is a peer. It might that you have now been promoted and need to have tough conversation with a friend and colleague, someone you socialise with. How do we manage this? Kim Parnell, Headteacher of Balfour Junior Academy in Medway, shared a great way to deal with this predicament. Try saying this at the start of the conversation, before your prepared opening sentence:

'This is not a conversation I would chose to have with you personally, but it is a conversation I need to have with you professionally.'

This sentence demarcates the friendship and professional relationship. It is crucial that you say it with meaning. I've heard it said like the mortgage disclaimer (the rushed 'Your home may be repossessed if you don't…') and when it's said in that perfunctory way it doesn't respect your friendship.

If you can have these kinds of conversations successfully with colleagues who are also your friends, you will find that your professional relationship will move to a higher level. You will cultivate professional respect and an ability to talk honestly with each other, as well as improving your friendship. These are tough conversations; however, I've seen the fruits of such labour many times and the marked improvement in professional relationships, as well as preserving friendships.

8. Raising issues at staff meetings that concern one or two people

This is a clanger. It's a mistake I see leaders make often and I'd like to help you avoid it.

Have you ever raised an issue with your whole staff, perhaps in a staff meeting or in an email, regarding something one or two people are doing or not doing? It might be reminding people of the marking policy (because two people aren't following it); it might be asking everyone to make sure they look professional at work (because a few people are a bit too casual); it might be reminding everyone that they need to check their emails regularly (because a couple of people are neglecting their email).

What typically happens is the people who are doing what you're asking hear the message and those who are not complying don't hear the message (or if they do, they don't act on it!)

My advice is to have the conversation with the specific people involved. It will be far more effective, and more likely to get the change you want. And it doesn't make everyone feel like they are being asked to do something they're already doing.

I was training a group of heads on successful difficult conversations. One of them informed us how a teacher had told the whole class off because of the behaviour of two children. Many of the children were upset at this and told their parents, who came in the next day to speak to the head. The heads in the group agreed this wasn't the way to deal with the issue, that the teacher should have spoken to the two children involved.

I asked the group if they had ever asked, in a staff meeting, for everyone to check their emails regularly. They had. I asked if this was really about a couple of people who were not checking their emails. They smiled knowingly and said 'yes'. I then asked: 'How was this any different to what the teacher did when they told off a whole class to reprimand a few children?' They gasped, and then laughed because they could see that it wasn't and that they needed to speak to the specific people in future.

9. The conversation gets heated

As we know, these conversations can get emotional. They can get heated very quickly and make it hard to think straight or manage our feelings, because it can trigger Parent or Child ego states for both people. Manage this by slowing down the conversation. The other person might be talking loudly, possibly angrily, so take long pauses before answering, where appropriate. You can give yourself permission to be silent by using phrases such as:

- 'I just need a moment to think.'
- 'I'd like to reflect on what you've said for a moment.'
- 'Will you give me a minute to think about this?'

If you respond as rapidly as they are talking, the conversation will escalate and get more heated, even frenetic, with both of you being in Parent or Child states and the conversation ending unsatisfactorily.

10. The nearest thing to a panacea in difficult conversations

Silence.

It really is golden.

And it can help your difficult conversations more than almost anything else.

Silence is the nearest thing to a panacea I've found. Of course, there needs to be dialogue and there needs to be a clear opening sentence but, once you're into the conversation, silence is one of the best, possibly *the* best, tool you have.

When should you use silence?

- When the other person is talking.
- When you need time to think.
- When the other person is thinking (out loud or in their head).
- After you've landed one of those great, Level 3 (see Figure 18) learning questions.
- When you don't know what else to say.
- When the conversation doesn't seem to be moving forward.
- After you, or they, have said something important.

I've seen silence act as the precious key that guides the conversation onto the path to success countless times.

I was working with a school leader who needed to tackle lateness with a TA. While this is typically at the easier end of the difficult conversation spectrum, it was actually a lot harder than anticipated because this lateness had not been picked up for a very long term (over a decade!) and this TA was quite fiery in her response.

When we practised (with an actor) the TA became like a 'resistant child' and the school leader would respond to almost everything the TA said. What he said was good, but it served only to fuel the fire within the TA and the conversation spiralled off track. We started the conversation again, this time with the school leader really working on listening and holding the silence. The effect was dramatic. The TA essentially burnt her anger out. She said what she wanted to say. The school leader didn't respond to everything, but visibly listened. The conversation became calmer and a simple dialogue brought it to a good conclusion. The school leader could see how powerful allowing silence could be.

Some of these problems might be familiar to you and I hope you find the tools I've offered useful. The landscape of a difficult conversation is rocky and to navigate the terrain with success you need to adapt as you move through the obstacles. I hope these tools will help you navigate the path to success.

Chapter 11: The legal side of difficult conversations

by Emma Webster, Employment Solicitor
and Joint CEO at YESS Law

In this chapter, we learn about:
· The five fair reasons for dismissal.
· Managing performance or 'capability'.
· Top tips and mistakes in managing performance.

This chapter is intended to give you a brief outline of how to manage poor performance fairly and lawfully. I will set out the basic legal parameters within which you must work, and identify some top tips and pitfalls.

The content of this chapter is not a substitute for legal advice. The challenge of employment law is that every scenario is fact specific; therefore, any legal advice will depend on those facts. This is an overview of the legal context you're working within and how to apply it[1].

Poor performance is often left unchallenged by 'managers until it has become a major issue. The reasons behind this are varied. It is very difficult to tell someone that they're not doing their job properly. It often feels like you're attacking that individual personally. Sometimes you will have inherited the problem. Occasionally, you'll be dealing with a

---

1 Legal situation as of the date of writing (August 2017).

difficult individual. Perhaps there are underlying health issues (in which case you may need to make allowances). However, you cannot leave the situation to fester. Doing so encourages bad practice, which in turn makes it more difficult to change.

Done properly, performance management should result in you retaining members of staff and making them more productive. It will save you the hassle, time, costs and risks of recruiting and training someone new. It will avoid potentially having to end someone's professional career. You should approach performance management on the basis that the person will improve; otherwise, you are likely to make mistakes.

One poor performing member of staff can have a disproportionately negative impact on the rest of the school and on their manager's time and stress levels. Fear of making 'legal' mistakes in the management of the situation can prevent people from taking appropriate action, which further exacerbates the problem. The aim of this chapter is to give you the confidence to approach each situation fairly and promptly.

An overview of unfair dismissal

If you unfairly dismiss someone, you expose your school to the risk of an employment tribunal claim, which costs time, money and causes a huge amount of stress. So, avoiding it should be high on your list of priorities when managing staff.

An employee with less than two years' continuous employment does not have the right to bring an unfair dismissal claim, except in certain limited circumstances. So, if an employee has less than two years' employment they have far fewer rights and may not be able to challenge your decision to dismiss them. Remember to check whether your employee has continuous employment with the local authority (if they've moved between schools). They might have been at your school for less than two years but, if their employment with the authority is greater than two years, they do have the right to an unfair dismissal claim.

However, you should be aware that an employee with less than two years' continuous employment can challenge a dismissal if:

- The decision to dismiss them or the circumstances around the dismissal are discriminatory under the Equality Act 2010.

- The decision has occurred because the employee has 'blown the whistle'.
- The decision was made because of trade union activities.

The characteristics that are protected under the Equality Act are:

- Age.
- Race/nationality.
- Religion or belief.
- Gender or sexual orientation.
- Pregnancy.
- Maternity.
- Disability.

There are other automatically unfair dismissal scenarios where an employee does not need two years' service, but that would be too much detail for this chapter. If in doubt, seek advice.

If you do unfairly dismiss someone, and they bring a successful tribunal claim, the school will have to pay damages made up of the person's net loss of earning. If discrimination has played a part, you will also have to pay an award for damage to their feelings. It will also cost you a lot in solicitors' fees, time, stress and, possibly, reputational damage among other staff.

An overview of fair dismissal

An employer can fairly dismiss an employee for one of five potentially fair reasons:

- Redundancy.
- Conduct.
- Capability.
- Lack/loss of qualification or statutory ban.
- Some other substantial reason (SOSR).

Below are the definitions for each. This chapter only deals with one aspect of capability dismissals in detail (that is poor performance capability dismissal as opposed to long-term sickness capability). Each reason has its own 'process' to follow for fair dismissal. Your school or local authority probably has separate policies for dealing with each issue and you should familiarise yourself with them.

Redundancy
This occurs where an employer requires fewer people to undertake work of a certain kind. For example, if you need to cut costs and reduce your reception/PA team from three to two, one role will be redundant.

Redundancy can be a complex area of law. The procedure required can be relatively detailed so I suggest seeking advice before embarking on a redundancy dismissal. Good, neutral sources of information are the ACAS website (www.acas.org.uk) and the BEIS website (www.beis.gov.uk).

Conduct
This is usually referred to as 'misconduct'. Conduct dismissals can arise where an employee continually misbehaves in a series of 'small' acts; for example, being late all the time. If, despite appropriate warnings, they continue to be late, provided that you follow a fair procedure, you can dismiss them fairly for the misconduct.

It is important to remember that deliberately refusing to carry out a reasonable management request can amount to misconduct. Sometimes it is difficult to tell the difference between someone actively refusing to do what a manager asks as opposed to not being capable of doing what a manager asks. It is really important to differentiate between the two because this will define which 'process' you follow when addressing the issue. I will come back to this in more detail in the 'Top tips' section later in this chapter.

Some examples of misconduct which Sonia and I have repeatedly come across in schools are:

1. Being rude to colleagues by ignoring them or repeatedly undermining them in meetings.

2. Refusing to take part in team meetings or remaining silent throughout.

3. Refusing to attend meetings with their managers.

4. Refusing to attend a one-to-one routine management meeting without a colleague as a 'companion'.

5. Repeatedly refusing to deliver lessons in the way they have been asked to, e.g. not adopting a new maths system of teaching that is being rolled out across the school.

Gross misconduct occurs where an employee's actions are so bad that they fundamentally breach the contract of employment. This is usually easy to spot – fighting with another member of staff, stealing, watching/ downloading inappropriate content online.

Capability

Capability covers any situation where somebody is no longer able to perform their role properly. This can occur either because someone is not good enough to do the work to the required standard, or if they are too unwell to work for a long period of time.

As this chapter deals with the process for fairly dismissing someone if they are not 'good enough' to perform their role to the required standard, I will not deal in any detail with long-term ill health dismissals. Schools normally have separate processes for dealing with long-term sickness absence. However, sometimes people who are in the process of being managed because they are performing badly for reasons unrelated to health, can become unwell (e.g. stress, anxiety, depression).

There is no magic answer to what you should do in those circumstances. You may consider adjusting time frames and targets if ill health occurs. If the employee is disabled, for the purposes of the Equality Act 2010, you must also make reasonable adjustments. If you are not sure if someone is disabled, refer them to an occupational health specialist to find out how you can help them and what adjustments you need to make.

If someone is not disabled but is unwell (for whatever reason), you may still need to consider progressing with a performance improvement plan, as and when the person attends work. If they are off for so long that you cannot complete the process, it is likely that they will end up being managed in accordance with your sickness absence policy. You should avoid cancelling any attempt to challenge poor performance because the person goes off sick every time the issue is raised.

Lack of qualification/statutory ban

This covers situations where continuing the employment is not legally possible. For example:

- Your caretaker has to drive between sites and loses their driving licence. If driving is an absolute requirement for their role, they probably cannot undertake it any more.

- One of your teachers requires a visa to work. The visa expires and the teacher forgets to apply for a renewal. To continue to employ them without the legal right to work is a criminal offence and you could face a fine of up to £10,000.

Some other substantial reason

This is a 'catch-all' category that covers situations which don't fit within the four above but can be justified as reasonable. Examples include:

- A significant breakdown in trust and confidence.
- Business reorganisation (short of redundancy).
- Refusal to accept changes to terms and conditions.
- Expiry of limited-term contracts.

Fairly managing poor performance (capability)

In a poor performance/capability dismissal, a tribunal will consider whether your decision to dismiss an employee for poor performance was within the range of reasonable responses based on a fair procedure. The fairness of that procedure depends on the circumstances, but is likely to take into account:

- The targets set.
- How long someone has been employed.
- The level of support and training offered to improve.
- The time frame given to improve.
- The transparency and clarity of the process.

Follow your procedure

Schools generally have a comprehensive performance management procedure. Unlike most other sectors, education has an extensive 'informal' process that you must follow before engaging with the formal process. An informal process means the part of the process where there is no threatened sanction (e.g. written warning or dismissal) if someone fails to improve (these are the difficult conversations Sonia is helping you with). Recent legislation states that where a teacher has been formally performance managed you **must** refer to this in any subsequent reference you provide for them – regardless of whether they 'passed' the process. This is likely to have a significant impact on how people approach performance management. The stakes are far higher for the individual involved at an earlier stage. It also means that they are less likely to resign and move on once you have started the formal part of the process because they are less likely to be able to find alternative work.

If possible, you should follow your internal procedure. If you need to deviate from it (e.g. change the time frame for when meetings occur) try to get the employee's agreement before doing so. There should be a good reason so that they have no reason to object. If they refuse to agree but you still need to change things, make sure you explain why and make sure your reasons are sound.

Significant deviation from a reasonable process and/or from your own internal process could lead to any dismissal being unfair. However, small changes to elements such as how long one part of the process takes will not render an entire process unfair. Tribunals will take an overview of the procedures followed and won't 'nitpick' over the tiny details. That said, it is usually easiest to follow your own internal procedures, where possible, to avoid that question being asked or any unnecessary disputes about process.

Basic step-by-step guide for formal capability

A basic performance management procedure should usually follow these steps.

1. **The manager should sit down and assess exactly what the performance problems are**

You should do this before you take any action or involve the employee. This is a private exercise. I believe that if you cannot write down what the person is/is not doing in a succinct list of bullet points, you will not be able to properly communicate the problem to them or set attainable targets. You should clearly identify what effect the performance issues are having, be it to colleagues, the children, on results etc. This list does not necessarily have to be shared with the person from the very beginning, but it is a way of identifying to yourself what must be communicated at some point to the person involved.

2. **Have an informal chat with that person to raise the problem(s)**

This is your first difficult conversation. Find out what they think is causing the situation. There may be facts (ill health, family crisis etc.) that you are not aware of. Respond appropriately, but say that the performance is a cause for concern and that you will be keeping an eye on it. Discuss ways of improving the situation. Offer help if necessary. You may have a number of these informal conversations where you are working with them to improve before you need to move to the next stage.

3. **If the informal chat does not work, and a reasonable period of time passes during which performance does not improve or does not improve enough, then write to the person, set out what the performance concerns are and invite them to a meeting to discuss it**

I suggest allowing them to be accompanied to this meeting by a trade union representative or a colleague, if they wish. Having a third party present can dispel any tension and provides a witness. It is very likely that your school's procedure requires you to allow them to be accompanied.

4. **Have a stage one formal meeting**

At the meeting find out what they think is causing the problems. Agree (if possible) on a performance improvement plan. The steps should be clear, reasonable and measurable, and with a set time frame during which they will be monitored.

Do not hold everyone to your own personal standards for work. You may well be able to do their job better but that is not what you should be measuring them against. The question is whether they are performing well enough to be a useful member of your team.

5. **Keep a note of all the meetings**

Get the notes agreed either at the end of the meeting or by sending a copy to them afterwards with a time frame for returning any amendments.

6. Agree the date for the next meeting

This helps avoid the process dragging on and ensures the person accompanying the employee to any meetings can also attend.

7. Write a letter/email after the meeting

Confirm what the performance issues are, the performance improvement plan that has been agreed/put in place, the targets they must meet and the date for the next meeting.

It should be clear at every meeting, and confirmed in every letter, what the possible repercussions of failing to reach the required level of performance will be. If the risk is that you will dismiss the person, you must be clear about that.

8. Hold a second meeting

If they have been successful and reached the targets, congratulate them. Find out what worked for them and why. Confirm that their performance must remain at this level and not slip again once all the support has ended. State that if their performance does slip in the near future, you will commence any performance management plan at this stage and not engage in an informal process first. This may not be appropriate if:

- The performance issues are different.

- A long time has passed.

- Your own internal performance management process differs; for example, it might stipulate that you cannot 'reopen' old processes or that they only remain on someone's record for a fixed period of time.

If they have not been successful, consider allowing them a final opportunity to improve, perhaps over a shorter time scale. If you decide to do this, you may decide to impose a sanction less than dismissal (i.e. a verbal warning, a written warning or a final written warning), repeat points 4–7 above and have a third meeting at the end.

If you do not feel that a further opportunity to improve is appropriate, you should consider whether it is reasonable to dismiss the person in all the circumstances. Relevant circumstances to consider are varied but include: whether you reasonably believe they can or will improve, the impact the poor performance is having, the size and resources of the school to support an under-performing member of staff and whether all options short of dismissal have been considered. If you decide that dismissal is an appropriate action, you should confirm this at the meeting. You will need to give them appropriate contractual notice (although, consider paying them in lieu of notice) that their employment will end.

9. Confirm your decision in writing with concise but thorough reasons

Depending on your process you may need to give them a right to appeal against any sanction (written warning, final written warning etc.). I strongly recommend that you give them the right of appeal against a dismissal even if your policy does not require it. The appeal should be heard by someone more senior than the person who made the decision to dismiss (e.g. a governor).

As stated above, I strongly believe you should approach this situation with the aim of improving someone's performance rather than dismissing them. Dismissing anyone for poor performance should always be the last resort. This is potentially the end of their career and never a decision that should be taken lightly or without you putting in a huge amount of effort to ensure that it is the only decision you can make for the benefit of the school.

Top tips

Always walk in their shoes

I believe that the best way to avoid making mistakes in this process is to approach it as if the person on the other side of the desk was you. How would you expect your employer to treat you if they had concerns? What would you want their response to be if you revealed a personal crisis or a health concern? What would you need from them to be able to address the performance concerns?

Remember that they have not spent the last half a term inside your head listening to your concerns about their performance or hearing the reports from other members of staff. Your conversation with them may be the first time they have had it raised directly. Even if it is not, it might be the first time they are being made aware of the potential consequences if they fail to change. That is stressful and upsetting for anyone.

Tackle the situation early

This solves so many problems. And it is what this book is all about: have these difficult conversations as early and as successfully as possible.

The individual has a genuine opportunity to rectify a problem if it has not become an embedded part of how they teach or work. They are more likely to be able to change.

The poor performance will have less of an impact on colleagues, children and parents.

It will be less emotive if you are not also dealing with stressed colleagues and under-achieving children.

As previously mentioned, an employee only has the right not to be unfairly dismissed if they have more than two years' employment (apart from some limited circumstances – see above) so the risk to the school from an early dismissal is far less than if you tackle it when they have been employed by you/your local authority for more than two years.

Common mistakes during capability

Dismissal should not come as a surprise to the employee

You will not have followed a fair process or managed the situation properly if, by the end of their final capability meeting, they do not realise that they are likely to be dismissed. This doesn't mean that you prejudge the outcome; it means that they should understand what they have to achieve in order to stay and can see for themselves when they haven't attained those targets.

Not keeping a note of all your meetings

There are inevitably disagreements or different interpretations of what was said or agreed at a meeting. Keeping an agreed note of the meetings avoids that becoming an issue.

Deciding to dismiss someone before you have given them a chance to improve

If you approach a capability dismissal with the intention to dismiss, you will set the person up to fail. Even if you think it is unlikely that they can improve, you must approach the process with the intention of trying to help them, not trying to dismiss them.

Confusing misconduct with capability

Sometimes this is a difficult call to make. Is someone refusing to work in a certain way because they do not want to or because they are not able to? It is probably misconduct if they do not want to work that way (or cannot be bothered). If they cannot work in that way, it is probably capability.

If you are not sure, I would suggest that it is usually best to approach it as a capability rather than a conduct issue. The process is less accusatory and gives the person an opportunity to change.

No joined up thinking between you and the employee's line manager

Ideally, the line manager will lead the process. However, this is not always appropriate or possible; for example, when a line manager doesn't have the skills to take someone through the process in a fair way and with the best chance of the individual improving. When it's not appropriate for the line manager to lead the process you need to get them on board first – they are critical to the success of any capability management. If they undermine the process by either helping or hindering the individual, the process is likely to be unfair, as you will not be able to properly assess their performance.

It may be that the line manager is conducting the performance management process themselves but at your instigation or with your support. In those situations, where you are not directly involved during the capability meetings, you will need to make sure that the line manager sufficiently understands your concerns and requirements.

Not giving a proper opportunity to improve

Send them on that course of action. Offer them one-to-one support and guidance. Create a 'Support and Challenge Plan'. Do what you think they need to really help them improve. Document all those steps. If that does not work, you will know that you are right to dismiss them.

Not setting realistic and attainable targets

Be careful not to hold them to your high standards. Try to secure their agreement about what is attainable. If it can't be agreed, record in writing why you think it is reasonable, and why they don't. Make the time frames realistic.

No teacher is going to be able to suddenly turn around a failing class in four weeks.

Conclusion

These tips and mistakes may sound obvious when they're set out in black and white but, from my experience, these mistakes are frequently made by managers. Tackling someone's poor performance can be very stressful for managers too. During times of stress, we often forget to take the basic steps before plunging into the middle of a procedure rather than starting carefully at the beginning. Hopefully, having read this chapter and combining it with everything Sonia advises about conducting successful difficult conversations, you will be able to consider and avoid the possible pitfalls.

Section 3

The bigger benefit of successful difficult conversations

Chapter 12: Creating a culture of feedback and improvement

In this chapter, we look at:
· The three things you can do with feedback.
· Giving quality feedback.
· How to role model receiving feedback.
· When feedback isn't feedback.

Giving and receiving feedback

Everything about successful difficult conversations pivots on constructive feedback. Feedback is a crucial factor in achieving high performance because your team cannot get there without it.

From lateness to rudeness, we're giving someone information about behaviour that does not meet the standard required. We are helping them improve. Expert feedback can go beyond incremental improvements to monumental improvements, leading someone from good into the realm of brilliant!

For high performance, we need a culture of feedback and, in this chapter, I share ways you can set about creating that extra pizzazz in your team, in addition to mastering successful difficult conversations.

Feedback is criticism

The problem is most people experience feedback as criticism, not as a welcome means of improvement. Despite the fact that we all know we're not perfect, it's not pleasant to be told we got something 'wrong'. It can feel like we are being criticised or having our faults pointed out. While feedback is essentially about learning, it's also about resilience. It can hurt when we realise we've got something wrong. This is a normal human reaction. But it's what we do with the feedback that counts.

Feedback is a gift

This is what one of the expert trainers at John Lewis told me and this piece of wisdom revolutionised how I saw and acted on feedback.

Feedback is a gift.

You have to take it.

But what you do with it is up to you.

You can:

Act on it, if you feel it is right.

Discard it, if you feel it is wrong.

Park it, if you're not yet sure. Maybe you want to wait to see if you receive other similar feedback in future and review your behaviour if you do.

We have a choice when we are given feedback. When we have a difficult conversation, we are showing someone their choices; choices they might not have been aware they were making. Bringing unconscious behaviour to their awareness allows them to make a conscious choice. As with any choice we make there are consequences – some better and some worse.

Feedback increases our self-awareness

The Johari window (Luft and Ingham, 1955) is an excellent model for explaining this.

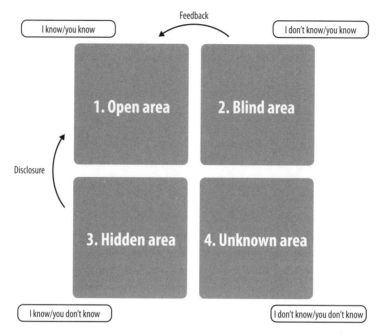

Figure 24: The Johari window (Luft and Ingham, 1955)

The window has four panes relating to four areas of self-awareness.

1. **The open area**

This is something I know about myself and you know about me: for example, you know I worked at John Lewis and I'm a qualified teacher.

2. **The blind area**

This is something you know about me, but I don't. Perhaps it's a habit I have that I'm unaware of or a phrase I keep using. A member of my team once told me that I fiddled with my rings sometimes, which made me appear nervous. I was unaware I was doing this and, in telling me, she moved this habit to my open area.

3. **The hidden area**

This is something I know about myself, but you don't. It's something I haven't chosen to disclose to you, for some reason. If I do, then this information will move to the open area, where we are both aware of it.

4. The unknown area

This is something I don't know about myself and you don't know about me until it is discovered. Think of this as an undiscovered talent.

> I had a boss who moved to a new John Lewis branch and, within a year, he'd secured a whole-branch refurbishment when his branch wasn't even on the refurbishment agenda. I marvelled as he told me about how he managed to do this and commented that I had no idea that he was so good at stakeholder management. He laughed and said neither did he, until now!

Giving and receiving feedback moves more knowledge into the open area so you become aware of it and can work on changing if you choose to. In difficult conversations we are usually moving the person's awareness from the blind area to the open.

Giving quality feedback

Giving good quality feedback is a skill built on a foundation of knowledge and experience. You might be great at giving feedback on lesson observations, but not so good when it comes to improving swimming technique if you're not a good swimmer yourself. Great feedback is very specific.

I love positive feedback (who doesn't?) but it frustrates me because often it's just not specific enough. Compliments like 'You were terrific today!' or 'You did a great job' are nice but not very useful, as such general statements don't tell us *why*. Break down *why* they were 'terrific' or 'great'. One or two specific points are all you need.

- 'The assembly was excellent because every child in your class was involved and it held the school's attention throughout.'
- 'Your displays are superb because they are educational (say how) and really draw the eye. I can't help but stop and look.'

It's even more important that constructive feedback in difficult conversations is very specific, as described in Chapter 5. People will not kick up a fuss if you simply say something was good or fabulous, but 'criticise' without specifics and you could you find yourself in a very tricky situation.

The sandwich

It's time to talk about that sandwich I mentioned briefly in Chapter 5.

To recap, the sandwich is essentially two pieces of positive feedback and one piece of constructive feedback sandwiched between the two. The idea is to acknowledge the good things the person is doing to provide some balance to the constructive feedback. The sandwich can help to 'soften the blow'.

I hate the sandwich.

I hate it because it undermines the positive feedback we are giving.

I hate it because it makes the conversation harder to have. If you've given great positive feedback and the person is glowing it's like you've built them up only to knock them down. That's painful for both of you.

I hate it because I think it trains us to only expect good feedback when there is bad feedback lurking. So, we don't hear the positives because we're waiting for the body blow!

Feel free to disagree with me and to use the sandwich if you find it works for you.

I'm not criticising anyone who uses this technique. I was trained in delivering feedback in this way and heard its virtues extolled. However, after sitting in quite a few meetings where I would dish up the bittersweet sandwich it became clear this unpopular snack wasn't working for me. So I threw out the sandwich to try other fresh approaches.

Despite my distaste for the sandwich, I think there is a place for positive and constructive feedback to live side by side in situations such as lesson observations or critiquing a report, which should be as balanced as possible. (If the lesson or report was dire it would be a more difficult conversation.)

Hit-and-run feedback

Hit-and-run feedback is something I like a lot. It only applies to positive feedback and can leave your team feeling a little confused, but in a good way. With this, you simply give positive feedback, with specifics, and then walk away. There is no constructive feedback to follow, just pure, positive feedback whenever you can give it.

If your team is used to the sandwich style of feedback, you might find they seem a little bewildered at first. This is because they were expecting the constructive feedback that never came.

Separating out the positive and constructive feedback is about keeping the feedback clean and pure.

Role model receiving feedback

It's one thing to give feedback but it's another to receive it well. Having a high-performing team requires a culture of feedback so you, as a leader in your school, need to role model receiving feedback well, to show how it is done so that others can learn. When given feedback:

1. **Say thank you** – show that you appreciate the feedback that has been given. This is always important, but even more so when it comes from someone who is below you in the hierarchy, as most people take a risk when they give upward feedback.

2. **Accept the feedback** – adopt a frame of mind that accepts the feedback as this will help you probe and understand it better. You might discard or park it later but, for now, entertain that there might be some gold nuggets in the comment and show a willingness to find them.

3. **Ask questions** – not everyone's feedback will be crisp and clear so you might need to ask some questions to understand it better. You might ask for some specific examples. It can help to position why you have questions by explaining: 'I'd like to understand this better and so I'd like to ask some questions about it, is that OK with you?' You don't want to sound like you're rejecting the feedback, you want to show that you're interested.

4. **Commit or don't commit** – remember that you have a choice with feedback: act on it, reject it or park it. If it's feedback that you know you want to act on then you can share that, but you might simply say that you want to take it away to consider what's been said.

5. **Show you're using it** – if you decide the feedback was useful and you want to act on it, show this where you can, in the same way you would want to see your team making use of feedback you've given to them.

Creating two-way feedback when you're the boss

Two-way feedback is important for our development, but the higher up you move the less *quality* feedback you can get. I know being a school leader, particularly a headteacher, can sometimes feel like being a punch bag from all angles, but these are rarely pieces of feedback that allow *you* to develop, they are often problems for you to fix.

You might have some great two-way feedback relationships with colleagues in your school already, those people who help you improve your own performance and conduct. You might want to develop some more and there are three ways to create more two-way feedback for you and your team.

Musical chairs

In one of my John Lewis branches our personnel manager shared this tool with our steering group and we loved it!

Once a month we'd play musical chairs.

We would pair up with each team member and share something we thought they did well and something we thought they could improve. We made sure both pieces of feedback were specific and had examples.

The good feedback felt exhilarating, while the constructive feedback felt helpful. Because the game included genuinely positive comments and observations about our blind spots, it didn't feel like the other person was being insincere in saying something good just so they could deliver something bad.

You might like to try this enjoyable activity with your SLT.

Ask two questions

I've seen this done via email with a bit of a preamble along the lines of 'I'm looking for feedback to help me know what I do well and see where I can improve. If you're willing to help me please can you answer these two questions.'

What can you rely on me for?

What can't you rely on me for?

Simple as that. You can ask colleagues, family or friends; any area of your life you would like to get feedback on. This can also be done via an anonymous response system through a 'post box' in the staffroom, to allow people to speak freely.

Capitalise on new team members

A golden opportunity to create two-way feedback culture is with new team members. Ask for feedback early into your working relationship and, when they give this to you, make sure you model receiving feedback and accept it unless it's poor quality feedback. Show them you welcome feedback. It may or may not be appropriate for you to give them feedback in that same meeting, that's a judgement call on your part. When you do give them feedback, model how to do it well. If their feedback is poor quality, explain to them that you'd like to be able to use their feedback and explain what would make their feedback easier to understand and act on. Encourage them to give feedback again.

You want to forge a great feedback relationship, which will help both of you develop.

I'm sorry to say that I have met heads, school leaders and governors who do not welcome feedback from their team and their schools suffer as a result of this defensive attitude. I've seen skilled individuals try to give upwards feedback, which was clearly unwelcome. It takes a lot of courage to do this and so someone must either really hate you, or really want the best for you and your school to muster the courage to give upwards feedback. In my experience, the latter motive is the more common.

It's important to have a few people who can give you valuable, perceptive feedback, even the stuff that is hard to hear, given on the basis of wanting to support you to do better in the future. These people have your back, so their feedback is never malicious, mischievous or just an opportunity to 'have a pop' at you.

Who will tell you what you don't want to hear?

I have a dear friend with whom I have an agreed 'licence to kill'. Not literally! We respect and care for each other and we only want the best for each other, to the point that we are willing to give each other feedback that is so hard to hear, but so important, that the person receiving it might not want to be friends anymore. This is our 'licence' to risk killing our friendship.

For us this is a declaration of how much we care for each other. We'll give each other the feedback that no one else will. We'll hold the mirror up when others wouldn't. And, if that means we no longer want to be friends, well, we love each other enough to say what needs to be said and accept the consequences.

This agreement might seem extreme and maybe one day it will end our friendship. Neither of us thinks it will, because we know whatever the feedback, it is given with the most loving intention of helping the other.

If you can have someone in your life, personal or professional, with whom you have a 'licence to kill' then you will have one of highest levels of feedback relationship there is, and that is something very special.

Activity 19: Who gives you the best feedback?

Take a moment to think about who, in your professional life, gives you quality feedback. Both the positive kind but also the tougher messages.

When feedback isn't feedback

Sometimes feedback isn't feedback: it's not aimed at helping you, it's aimed at making you feel bad. When this is the case there is usually a bigger reason behind the attack. It might be a relationship issue with the person, or even something like jealousy.

When this happens, role model receiving feedback because step 3 – asking questions – will show it for what it is. Feedback that is perhaps 'spiteful' often doesn't have examples to back it up, so ask for specific examples. If they have examples then there could be some truth to the feedback but, if not, then tell them you will park the feedback for now, because without any specific examples it's hard to fully understand it. However, if they think of an example in the future, tell them to let you know so that you can understand it better and decide if it's feedback you choose to act on.

This will show you are willing to improve but the quality of their feedback needs to improve for you to take it on board.

Closing remarks

Successful difficult conversations are an important leadership skill.

The issues you're dealing with cost time and money, they affect the impact your team can have and how great they can make the education you are providing to your students.

These issues are a barrier to school improvement and if you want your school to be great, or outstanding, you must learn to improve these issues around performance and conduct, quickly and kindly.

There's no one thing that makes a school great. There are many ingredients to it: a powerful vision, strategic decision-making, focusing on the right things at the right time, and many more. Successful difficult conversations are one of these ingredients. They are a hallmark of high-performing teams; teams who understand there is no failure, only feedback; teams who want to do what they do better than they were doing before. This is an improving school, a school with healthy conflict; a school with a culture of feedback.

What does a school with healthy conflict look like?
In a school with healthy conflict there isn't an absence of conflict altogether. Conflict and difficult conversations are seen and received as feedback. People know how to handle feedback when it is given and they are skilled at delivering it well. There is a welcome expectation of talking about what went well and what didn't, and this isn't about blame; it's about learning for the team and the individual, so they can do their best for their students.

Such a school is better at self-regulating and improving its performance and conduct. If someone isn't performing to the expected standard it will stand out and either they will improve themselves or others will help them. The same is true of conduct.

Developing people is the joy of leadership
I know leadership carries with it great responsibility and can lead to the dreaded '3am' wake up worries. However, I do believe leadership is a joy and a privilege; it's something I have always enjoyed. As someone who has been a successful class teacher, you know what it is to develop your team, to make a difference to their performance, their behaviour and their happiness. You've done it with classes of around 30 pupils; as a leader, you're doing the same thing with a team of adults. This joy of leadership is:

to develop everyone so that the whole is greater than the sum of the parts.

To do that, it's inevitable that you must have some difficult conversations. I hope this book will help you have them with less stress and more success.

Next steps

I've covered a lot in this book and I really hope it has helped you because, as a fellow teacher, I know difficult conversations are not why you do what you do but, as a fellow leader, we both know how important they are.

In fact successful difficult conversations is one of the ways we help headteachers create a genuinely outstanding school. Our schools get great results, many gaining or maintaining their outstanding judgement, but in a way that is true to what they believe education should be.

If you'd like to learn how you can do the same come to an event or webinar and let me help you further: https://ukheadsup.com/events/

Appendix A: Chapter summaries

Section 1: Why you should have difficult conversations	
Chapter 1: Conflict is crucial for great schools	The definition of a successful difficult conversation.
	Why difficult conversations are crucial for school improvement.
	The psychology behind team conflict.
Chapter 2: The cost of conflict	How much conflict is costing you in time and money.
Chapter 3: Picking your battles	Why difficult conversations are so hard.
	How to know if you should have a difficult conversation.
	Prioritising what difficult conversations are essential.
	Deciding *who* should have the conversation.
	Timing when to have the conversation.
Section 2: How to have successful difficult conversations	
Chapter 4: The three core components of a successful difficult conversation	The three common problems with difficult conversations.
	The three core components of successful difficult conversations.
Chapter 5: Getting the conversation started	The most common mistake made during difficult conversations and how to crack it.
	The only black-and-white rule of difficult conversations.
	How to start a conversation for success.
Chapter 6: Managing the emotions of difficult conversations	What is happening emotionally during difficult conversations.
	Changing the other person's behaviour.
	Reducing the emotional energy of difficult conversations.
Chapter 7: Ensuring the conversation creates positive change	How you are sabotaging yourself.
	How to reduce your workload in a difficult conversation.
	How to make positive change more likely to happen.
Chapter 8: Structuring the conversation for success	How to structure a difficult conversation.
	How to follow up in writing.
	What to do when a conversation comes at you and you haven't had time to prepare.
Chapter 9: Adapting your approach for success	Different approaches to increase the success of your difficult conversation.
	How to know which approach will work best.
Chapter 10: Ten common problems and how to avoid them	How to have a difficult conversation with a work colleague who is also a friend.
	What to do if you can't agree.
	How to deal with distractions.
	How to get someone to take the issue seriously and take action to improve it.
	The nearest thing to a panacea in difficult conversations.

Chapter 11: The legal side of difficult conversations by Emma Webster, Employment Solicitor and Joint CEO at Yess Law	The five fair reasons for dismissal. Managing performance or 'capability'. Tops tips and mistakes in managing performance.
Section 3: The bigger benefit of successful difficult conversations	
Chapter 12: Creating a culture of feedback and improvement	The three things you can do with feedback. Giving quality feedback. How to role model receiving feedback. When feedback isn't feedback.

Appendix B: All the activities

Activity 1: How many difficult conversations are you having?

Take a moment to think about how many difficult conversations have come at you and how many you need to have (whether you did or not).

How many difficult conversations have come your way this week? _____

How many difficult conversations should you have initiated this week (whether you did or not)? ___

Activity 2: The cost of conflict

School budgets are tight, and getting even tighter, and heads are expected to do more with less.

Conflict has many costs and the biggest cost is to your culture. Unresolved conflict also has some very real and tangible costs and there's a simple way to calculate the costs for your school.

Estimate how many hours per week are spent across your school on:

Difficult conversations.

Conflict.

Accountability conversations.

Gossip.

Talking about staff performance or conduct.

Performance improvement meetings (not your planned annual performance meetings).

Take that number and complete this sum:

_____ X 40 weeks = _____ X £25 p/hour* = _____

Hours per week Annual time   Annual cost

*This is a weighted average hourly rate across a range of roles.

Activity 3: Go online for an accurate cost of conflict

You can get a more accurate calculation of the cost of conflict in your school with my easy-to-fill-in spreadsheet and short video. It will take you about five minutes. Go to: www.ukheadsup.com/resources/want-to-work-out-how-much-conflict-is-costing-your-school/

Activity 4: Why are difficult conversations so hard?

Take a moment to think about why you find difficult conversations so hard.

Stop, and before reading further, list at least two main reasons why.

Activity 5: Who and what difficult conversations do you have?

If you have a few difficult conversations that need to be tackled (by you or your wider team) then it can be useful to jot down the cases you are aware of. These could include conversations with teachers, parents, governors, employees at the local authority, an academy or a MAT.

Who	Issue with their performance or conduct? (P or C)	What is it specifically about?	Importance rating (1 not very, 4 critical)

I realise this could be sensitive information so only write it down if you're comfortable, otherwise just think it through.

Activity 6: Go online to know which is the best box to focus on

The best box on the grid to focus on is Box 8. If you'd like to know more go online to www.ukheadsup.com/performancebehaviourmatrix/

Activity 7: Who has the majority of difficult conversations?

1) Tick which statement best applies to your school:

The head has the majority of difficult conversations.

The SLT has most of the difficult conversations.

Middle/phase/year group leaders have the majority of difficult conversations.

Everyone at our school is good at having the difficult conversations they need to have and only take issues to more senior staff when necessary.

2) Put a star next to the statement you *want* to have.

If you've ticked and starred the same statement then let's have a virtual high-five!

If you've ticked and starred number four let's have a virtual high-ten!

Activity 8: Is it worth the extra time?

How many conversations have you had about this so far? _____

How much time have you spent on this issue so far? _____

(If you haven't spoken to them yet, estimate the time).

How effective has it been in resolving the issue on a scale of one to ten? (1 low, 10 high) ___

Towards the end of the training I ask them:

How many conversations do you think you will now need to resolve this issue? _____

How long do you think these conversations will take if you use the skills I've taught you? ___

How effective do you think it will be in resolving the issue? (1 low, 10 high) _____

You can then compare the two and make an informed choice as to whether you continue as you have been or try the approaches I've given you.

Activity 9: What is the biggest problem for you?

Think of up to five recent difficult conversations you've had that didn't go well and enter them in the table below. Tick the problems you experienced.

Conversation	1. Didn't hear my message	2. It got emotional	3. Didn't make changes	Other
1				
2				
3				
4				
5				

Circle the most common problem in your difficult conversations.

Activity 10: What issues do you experience because of the start of your conversation?

Do any of these outcomes sound familiar to you? Highlight the ones you have experienced. Put a star next to the one you have experienced the most.

Most of the time when the other person walks away not having heard the message you wanted to convey, it's usually because *you* haven't been clear enough, not because *they* haven't listened.

Activity 11: Your opening sentence

Think of a difficult conversation you need to have and write down your opening sentence the first time. Now apply tips and look out for the traps above and improve it. Try to improve your sentence at least four times.

Activity 12: Watch TV

Pick a show you enjoy and next time you watch it see if you can work out which of Berne's ego states the characters are in.

Activity 13: What games are you playing?

Think about some of the difficult conversations you've had. What roles did you and the other people take on? Is there one role you find yourself in more often than others?

Activity 14: Go online to see how to manage negative body language

Go to www.ukheadsup.com/negativebodylanguage/ where I'll show you how to positively mirror negative body language (a far better medium than explaining in writing).

Activity 15: Practise building rapport in a safe space

To help you be more aware of low-cost practise opportunities going forward, take a moment to think of two low-cost opportunities you've recently had where you would have been able to practise your rapport skills.

Activity 16: Go online to learn more about the STORM structure

You can access a free, short video e-course taking you through the STORM structure at www.ukheadsup.com/storm/

Activity 17: What approach do they need from me?

Think of a difficult conversation you need to have. You might like to use ones you thought about for **Activity 5**: Who and what difficult conversations do you have? on page 43.

Apply the skill/will matrix to see what approach you think will work best in that difficult conversation.

Who	Issue with their performance or conduct? (P or C)	What is it specifically about?	Importance rating (1 not very, 4 critical)	Skill: High or low	Will: High or low	Approach

Activity 18: What are your most common problems?

It helps to know which problems you experience most during difficult conversations. Look at the list below and self-assess which of them you experience most, by highlighting the three most common for you.

1. They don't hear what I want them to hear.

2. They always change the subject.

3. They agree with me, but don't take any action to change.

4. We don't agree and can't move forward.

167

5. They ask, 'Who told you that?', but I can't tell them.

6. Having a difficult conversation with a colleague who is also a friend.

7. At staff meetings the only people who don't respond to issues are the people who need to!

8. The conversation gets heated or emotional.

9. They say nothing and keep silent.

Activity 19: Who gives you the best feedback?

Take a moment to think about who, in your professional life, gives you quality feedback. Both the positive kind but also the tougher messages.

Appendix C: A table of figures

Appendix D: Successful difficult conversations checklist

Structure:	Done
What do you want to achieve from the conversation?	
What do you want to talk about?	
What outcome do you want? (Focus on what goal you want to achieve, not the method of achieving it.)	
Why is this an issue?	
What examples of this specific behaviour or issue do you have? (Aim for three.)	
What are your feelings and how will you separate them from the issue?	
Have you written your opening sentence? Have you changed/clarified foggy words? Have you removed as many big words (more than three syllables) as possible? Have you improved it four to five times? Have you checked it with someone else?	

Emotions:	
How are they likely to respond? (Parent/Adult/Child? Positive/negative?)	
How are you likely to respond? (Parent/Adult/Child? Positive/negative?)	
Do you need an adult phrase or reframe to put you in a good state of mind for the conversation?	
In the meeting – build trust	
Stance: Sit like they sit.	
Say: Use their words.	
Signal: Use their gestures.	
Summarise: What they have said.	
Logistics	
When is the best time to have the conversation?	
Make sure you have a suitable location for the meeting.	
Know how long you have for the conversation and allow some time to overrun.	
If you need a break, do you know what options you have?	
After the meeting	
Do you need any HR or legal advice?	
Send a written summary of the meeting.	
Clarify when you will follow up.	
If it was an emotional meeting, touch base with them within 24 hours.	

Works cited

Berne, E. (1964). *Games People Play: The Psychology of Human Relationships*. New York: Grove Press.

Covey, S. R. (2004). *The 7 Habits of Highly Effective People*. London: Simon & Schuster.

Cuddy, A. (2012, June). Your Body May Shape Who You Are. [video] Accessed at www.ted.com/talks/amy_cuddy_your_body_language_shapes_who_you_are.

Department for Education [DfE] (2011). Teachers' standards. London: Department for Education. Accessed at www.gov.uk/government/publications/teachers-standards.

Groundhog Day. (1993). [film] Hollywood, Harold Ramis.

Landsberg, M. (2003). *The Tao of Coaching*. London: HarperCollins.

Luft, J. and Ingham, H. (1955). *The Johari window, a graphic model of interpersonal awareness. Proceedings of the western training laboratory in group development*. Los Angeles: UCLA.

Mehrabian, A. (1981). *Silent messages: Implicit Communication of Emotions and Attitudes*. Belmont, CA: Wadsworth.

Robbins, T. (2012) *Unlimited Power: The New Science of Personal Achievement*, Simon and Schuster

Tuckman, B. W. (1965). Developmental sequence in small groups. *Psychological Bulletin*, 63(6), 384-399.